GOING HOME

Building Peace in El Salvador:
The Story of Repatriation

LAURA JACKSON: *Packing to go home.*

QUE VIVA the refugees,
    and may they truly LIVE!
QUE VIVA the refugees in the place of their birth,
    and may they truly LIVE!
    cry the people.
But really let them live, cry the people.

In El Salvador,
    cry the people.
Without the bombing,
    cry the people.
Without mortars,
    cry the people.
Without relocation,
    cry the people.
Without forced relocation,
    cry the people.

QUE VIVA the refugees,
    and may they truly LIVE!
    cry the people.
QUE VIVA the refugees in the place of their birth,
    and may they truly LIVE!
    cry the people.

In Honduras,
    cry the people.
In Costa Rica,
    cry the people.
In Nicaragua,
    cry the people.
In El Salvador,
    cry the people.
All over the world,
    cry the people.

(Part of a song cycle from Santa Marta, one of the repatriated villages.)

GOING HOME

Building Peace in El Salvador:
The Story of Repatriation

Compiled and edited by Vic Compher and Betsy Morgan
Photography editor: Laura Jackson

The Apex Press
New York and London

Going Home: Building Peace in El Salvador is first being published by The Apex Press, 777 United Nations Plaza, New York, New York 10017, USA (212/953-6920) and 57 Caledonian Road, London N1 9BU, U.K. (071/837-4014)

Library of Congress Cataloging-in-Publication Data:

Going home : building peace in El Salvador, the story of repatriation / compiled and edited by Vic Compher and Betsy
    Morgan : photography editor, Laura Jackson.
        p. cm.
    Includes bibliographical references.
    ISBN 0-945257-21-X
    1. Refugees—El Salvador. 2. Refugees—Honduras. 3. Repatriation—El Salvador. 4. Refugees—El Salvador—
Pictorial works. 5. Refugees—Honduras—Pictorial works. 6. Repatriation—El Salvador—Pictorial works. I. Compher,
Vic, 1945- . II. Morgan, Betsy, 1943- . III. Jackson, Laura.
    HV640.5.S24G65 1991
    362.87′097284—dc20
                                         91-10917
                                           CIP

BritishLibrary Cataloguing-in-Publication Data:

Going home : building peace in El Salvador.
    I. Compher, Vic. 1945-   . II. Morgan, Betsy, 1943-
    972.84053

    ISBN 0-945257-21-X

Book layout and design by Peggy Hurley
Cover design by Jim Gerhard; photo by Harvey Finkle (*Refugees leave Mesa Grande during the fourth repatriation*)
Typeset and printed in the United States of America

We gratefully acknowledge the support of the Funding Exchange/Phoebus Fund toward the completion of this book.

Proceeds will be contributed to the support of the economic and social development projects in the repopulated villages of El Salvador through the SHARE Foundation.

CONTENTS

ADAM KUFELD: *On the bus from Mesa Grande to El Salvador, October 10, 1987.*

STEVE CAGAN: *"The permanent solution for refugees is to repatriate ourselves in community."*

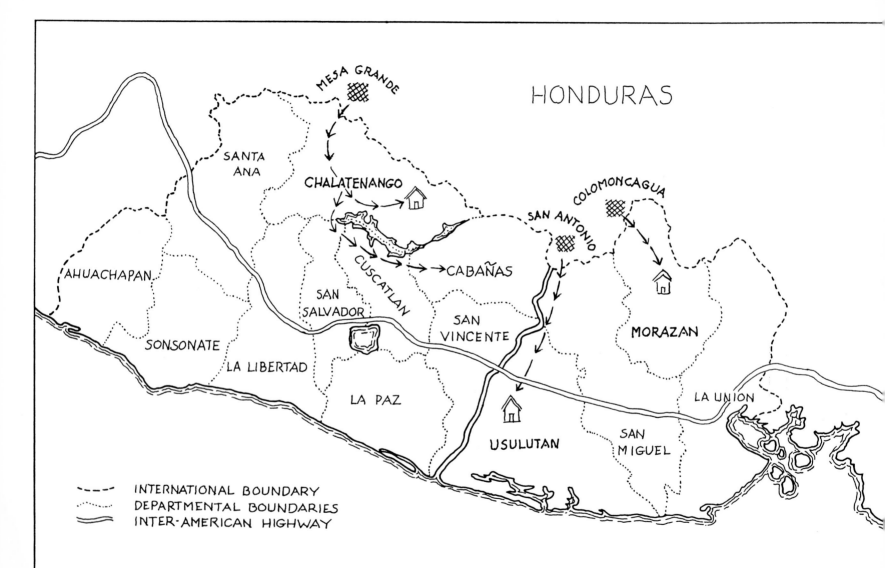

HONDURAS

MESA GRANDE

SANTA ANA

CHALATENANGO

COLOMONCAGUA

SAN ANTONIO

AHUACHAPAN

SANTA ANA

CUSCATLAN

CABAÑAS

SAN SALVADOR

SAN VINCENTE

MORAZAN

SONSONATE

LA LIBERTAD

LA PAZ

USULUTAN

SAN MIGUEL

LA UNION

- - - INTERNATIONAL BOUNDARY
········· DEPARTMENTAL BOUNDARIES
～～～ INTER-AMERICAN HIGHWAY

M

INTRODUCTION:
THE EXILE AND THE RETURN

In fulfillment of a long-held dream, 4,313 men, women, and children left the Mesa Grande refugee camp in Honduras in an enormous caravan of buses and trucks on October 10 and 11, 1987, to repatriate in their native El Salvador. Indeed it was the first and, to this day, the largest mass repatriation in the history of Latin America. Three other large groups from Mesa Grande, totaling about 4,000, joined the movement home in the summer of 1988 and the fall of 1989. Over 9,000 refugees from the camps at Colomoncagua and San Antonio returned to El Salvador in the winter of 1989-90.

Despite enormous struggles with the Honduran, Salvadoran, and United States governments, and with the United Nations High Commission for Refugees, these Salvadorans, in the spirit of celebration and victory and through sheer faith and conviction, returned to their country to reclaim and to rebuild the destroyed towns from which they had been driven some nine years before. They could no longer wait for the seemingly interminable civil war to end, but returned to El Salvador in order to reestablish "zones of peace."

At the request of the refugees themselves, each of the repatriating groups was accompanied by international delegations from Catholic and Protestant churches in the United States, Canada, and Western Europe; by representatives of Jewish communities; and always by the very visible leaders of churches in El Salvador, especially the Catholic, Episcopal, Lutheran, and Baptist churches. In the presence of these supporters, the elected leaders of the refugees, known as the *directiva*, negotiated vigorously to establish the safe conditions for each of the now legendary *retornos*. They also organized the vast number of trucks and buses and the considerable supplies needed for these journeys.

The refugee community's solidarity, self-determination, faith, and hope are qualities which have been noted again and again by those accompanying them. As one of the North American delegates so aptly observed:

> It was the pride of this refugee community that was so astounding. In the caravan there were two symbols of this pride: the lead bus with the music, and the tractor. When, after extended negotiations and a night spent sleeping on the side of the road, the convoy finally crossed the border, it was the blue and white Ford tractor that got the loudest cheers. It drove through the ranks of Salvadoran soldiers, armed with automatic rifles, and beneath the two US Army helicopters which had been circling the convoy. Our tractor against your guns! Our will to farm again in our own land against your military strategies!

This book is written first and foremost as a tribute to the refugees. It provides an opportunity for them to tell their compelling stories and for the internationals who accompanied them to bear witness to truly historic events.

But before you encounter the interviews, stories, and photographs that make up this tribute, it is important to understand how these people came to be refugees in the first place, their experiences in the camps for nearly a decade, and how they prepared themselves to do the seemingly impossible—namely, to return as emissaries of peace to the very war zones where they had suffered persecution less than ten years before.

The decade of the 1970s saw a remarkable upsurge of organized resistance to economic oppression by the poor in El Salvador. People in Christian-base communities, enlightened by scripture and looking at the lopsided distribution of wealth that characterized Salvadoran society, concluded that it was not God's will that they should always suffer. These same poor people formed the new labor unions, the organizations of shantytown dwellers in the cities, and the organizations of *campesinos* (people who work on the land). Organizations, such as the Federation of Christian Campesinos (FECCAS) and the Union of Rural Workers (UTC), came into conflict with the government as they held demonstrations and, at times, occupied uncultivated land.

The armed revolutionary groups, which were eventually to form the Farabundo Marti National Liberation Front (FMLN), also developed during the 1970s. Not much is known about the relationship between these parallel developments. However, an alliance between most of the popular organizations and the guerrillas became explicit in April 1980, with the formation of the Democratic Revolutionary Front (FDR), a coalition of opposition organizations which included the merged FECCAS-UTC. By that time, the conflict between the guerrilla armies and the military-dominated government of El Salvador had escalated to full-scale civil war. For the government armed forces, however, the enemy was not only the guerrillas. The army conducted a campaign of extermination against civilian opponents of the status quo as well.

Among the principal targets of this campaign was the rural population wherever FECCAS and UTC were strong. These regions included the northern departments of San Vicente, Chalatenango, and Cabañas, which border on Honduras.

Beginning in December 1979, the army, National Guard, Treasury Police, and ORDEN (a civilian paramilitary group) invaded villages, rounded up *campesino* organizers—as well as their families in some cases—and tortured and killed them. By early March 1980, Amnesty International received reports that "hundreds of *campesinos* in the villages supporting opposition labor organizations in Morazan, Cuscatlan, Chalatenango, and San Salvador departments" had been killed or had disappeared (Amnesty International 4-5). In a news release on March 17, 1980, Amnesty revealed that "in Chalatenango department, a circle of fire was lit around a village to prevent local people escaping; troops then entered the village, killing some 40 people and abducting many others." Other witnesses have described the bombing and strafing of villages by military helicopters (Carmada 15, 17). The result was the displacement of thousands of people in the countryside, some fleeing to the towns and cities, while others crossed the border into Honduras.

Even as they fled, they were targets. On May 14, 1980, 1,200 panic-stricken *campesinos*, who were being pursued by the armed forces, attempted to cross the Sumpul River into Honduras. Instead of finding safe haven on the other side, they were met by Honduran troops who started firing on them, thereby driving them back into the gunfire of the advancing Salvadoran forces. Approximately 600 of these people, primarily women, children, and elderly people who could not swim across the swollen river, were massacred.

Tragically, such atrocities against civilians, especially of the northern and eastern provinces, occurred again and again. At the Lempa River on March 17 and 18, 1981, 4,000 fleeing persons, primarily women and children, were fired on by Salvadoran and Honduran troops, killing over 70. And again at the Sumpul River, on May 30, 1982, 10 percent of the 2,000 civilians trying to escape the military forces of both countries were murdered (Carmada 19-21, 81, 83, 85).

By July of 1980, there were already nearly 16,350 internal Salvadoran refugees. Within five years these numbers had swelled to 500,000. At the same time, documented bombing attacks on the people had increased from 111 in 1982 to over 1,600 by 1985. By the end of the decade, over 73,000 persons, mostly civilians, had been killed almost entirely by various branches of the Salvadoran armed forces or by the paramilitary death squads linked to them. In addition, 1.5 million had been displaced out of a population of 5 million in a country with the land mass of Massachusetts and 600,000 to 700,000 of these displaced persons continued to live in El Salvador, usually in refugee camps or impoverished *barrios* around urban areas. A half-million refugees fled to the United States, 200,000 to Mexico, 23,000 to Nicaragua, 24,000 to Honduras, and 100,000 to other Central American countries (*A Dream Compels Us* 205-207).

The survivors of this "scorched earth policy" and of the massacres described above are the people about whom this book is written. During 1980, 5,000 of these people hung onto survival just inside the Honduran border, largely through the help of sympathetic Honduran civilians and church relief teams, primarily CARITAS and Catholic Relief Services, CEDEN (a coalition of Evangelical groups), the Mennonite Church, and several other humanitarian organizations. Between late 1980 and the spring of 1981, the United Nations High Commission on Refugees (UNHCR) established refugee camps for these and other arriving refugees in three places near the Salvadoran/Honduran border: La Virtud, Colomoncagua, and San Antonio. La Virtud and Colomoncagua housed between 5,000 and 6,000 each (Carmada 81, 83).

Life in all three camps was extremely harsh. In addition to overcrowding, there were insufficient potable water, meager food supplies, poor sanitation, and even poorer protection from the elements. Disease and malnutrition were rampant. Most alarming, however, was the Salvadoran and Honduran armies' freedom to enter and search the camps with impunity and to take captives whom they tortured, killed, or "disappeared."

The UNHCR seemed to be either incapable or unwilling to relieve these conditions. Under considerable pressure from the Honduran, Salvadoran, and US governments, who were thought to be trying to create a potential staging area for their own military forces, the commission forcibly relocated the refugees of La Virtud 50 kilometers from the border. The refugees vigorously resisted this move because they did not trust the military forces that would oversee the move,

and they did not want to be separated further from their homeland and their prospects of returning home. They were finally moved on the assurances that they would be safer and that living conditions would be more comfortable.

When the first 1,200 refugees from La Virtud arrived on the broad plateau near San Marcos, which was called Mesa Grande, they were disillusioned to find a flat wooded area without any infrastructure: no tents, no water, no latrines, no cooking stoves. Thus, they, and those who arrived later, were forced to clear the land and to build the entire camp. By mid-April 1982, all of the refugees—a total of 7,000—had been moved from La Virtud. In this traumatic move, 22 people were murdered and 16 "disappeared" by the military of both El Salvador and Honduras (Carmada 84-85). Mesa Grande camp, with adequate space for only 2,000 refugees, had over 12,000 by the mid-1980s.

Surrounded by barbed wire, the people were unable to come and go at will and often had trouble receiving international visitors. They continued to be harrassed by the Honduran military. In the first year of Mesa Grande's existence, there were over 100 reports of adults and children captured and tortured by the Honduran military, usually as they were near the edges of the camp collecting wood or working in the fields that they were allowed to plant (Carmada 86). Such assaults and disappearances occurred until the late 1980s, although not as frequently, giving all three camps more the aura of concentration camps or prisons than safe havens.

It is all the more significant, then, that the refugees, having suffered such abuses both before and after their entry into the camps, created highly supportive and democratic communities within the camps in order to secure a more productive life for their children and themselves. They were quick to form grassroots faith groups (Christian-base communities) in which they tried to interpret the circumstances of their lives in the context of the Bible. Each camp democratically elected a *directiva* or council, which made decisions and spoke on behalf of the refugees in their negotiations with the various powers they needed to confront. Likewise, the refugees organized themselves into block groups of about ten families each, with designated individuals for each block who would equitably distribute food, essential supplies, and many items produced in the camps.

With the help of humanitarian organizations, the refugees developed a number of quite productive workshops or cooperatives. These included groups to produce hammocks, clothing, shoes, ceramics, embroidery and other crafts, tin and iron ware, and the like. According to the UNHCR, more than one-third of the adults were engaged in these cottage industries, while most of the others were involved in agriculture, construction, and a variety of health and educational services within the camps (Carmada 98). Many of the teachers in the schools were refugees who had been trained by professional teachers sent by CARITAS. As a result of self-run preschools and child and basic adult educational programs, literacy climbed from 15 percent in the early 1980s to 85 percent by 1989 (Schmidt 3). Health workers trained numerous refugee health promoters, who, in turn, created special training programs for other refugees. Therefore, despite the context of military repression and the harsh reality of an unsteady supply of UNHCR materials, international visitors to the camps found a highly industrious, motivated, and well-organized refugee population, with an astute and articulate leadership.

The development of community life and the acquisition of productive skills have served these people well as they have confronted continual threats and challenges during their nine years in the camps. After the traumatic relocation of the La Virtud community to Mesa Grande, the UNHCR, under pressure from the Honduran, Salvadoran, and US governments, continued to plan for further massive relocations of all three camps into the interior of Honduras. During the mid-1980s, announcements of these plans with dates for actual moves were very distressing to the refugees who from experience could only envision the demise of their considerable developmental gains. They were especially concerned about being forcibly dispersed into small segregated hamlets in the proximity of US and Honduran military bases (Carmada 89-91). Therefore, they initiated an active and ultimately successful campaign against such plans, using international agencies and visitors as their witnesses to the world community. Church constituencies in El Salvador as well as in the United States, Canada, and Western Europe proved to be their most influential allies.

In addition to the relocation issue, the refugees and many internationals continued to protest recurring violence by the Honduran military toward refugees; the Honduran government's threat to take over administration of their schools and health and workshop programs; and the UNHCR's various budgetary cutbacks which would have crippled these programs ("Salvadoran Refugees in Honduras" 21, 28).

Dependent in large measure upon the UNHCR for their basic resources, the refugees found that it was necessary to maintain working relationships with this agency, while continuing to cultivate more significant connections with church and humanitarian groups. In relation to the UNHCR, the *directivas* developed an assertive though diplomatic style that included nonviolent protest and appeal. Direct actions included meetings, sit-ins, demonstrations, songs, fasts, banners, and chants, as the occasion seemed to require and depending on the tone and leadership style of any of the camps at a given time.

Certainly one of the greatest challenges and eventual opportunities to come to the refugees was the idea of repatriation itself—an idea which in its original form in the mid-1980s was perceived to be a counterinsurgency strategy of the Salvadoran and US governments. Under the original plan, which was to be financed largely by US AID, the Salvadoran government would establish designated villages for returning refugees that would be effectively monitored by security forces. These proposed hamlets placed the refugees in areas of El Salvador that were a considerable distance from friends and relatives, thereby dispersing the community, which the Salvadoran government identified (and continues to identify) with the popular movements of the country, especially the FMLN guerrillas. Most of all, the refugees were concerned that these villages would subject their youth to conscription into the military and lead to persecution of those who could not support the government. Not surprisingly, the refugees lobbied vigorously against this plan of so-called "voluntary repatriation" (*A Dream Compels Us* 208; "Salvadoran Refugees in Honduras" 1-11).

Meanwhile in El Salvador, the 1980s witnessed a political and military stalemate. Neither the juntas of the early 1980s, the provisional government of 1982 to 1984, nor Duarte's administrations thereafter were able to stop the regressive behavior of the military. At the same time, these governments could not hold back the irrepressible organizing efforts of the popular movements which reemerged in the mid-1980s. Although the nearly half dozen elections between 1982 and 1989 were used by the United States to attempt to "certify democracy," the opposition contended that without a prior negotiated settlement to the war and the establishment of an enforceable cease-fire, they could not participate safely, and the election could not truly be a free election. While the extreme right-wing ARENA party, which had gained control in 1988 and 1989, tried to echo some of the popular sentiment which pressed for negotiations, the government with the full support of US military and economic aid, reaching 1.5 million dollars daily (and 4 billion dollars for the decade), had no incentive to change from their longstanding objective for total military victory. At the same time, the FMLN pressed for negotiations by trying to make the country essentially ungovernable (Berryman 1, 3).

For the refugees, watching the war drag on year after year, it no longer seemed sensible simply to endure life in virtual concentration camps until peace came to their land. Despite their suspicion of the government's talk of "voluntary repatriation," they were quite interested in reports concerning early repopulation efforts by displaced persons from within El Salvador. The first large-scale, organized internal repopulation took place as early as January 1986 in Tenancingo, Cuscatlan, as a result of successful negotiations by Archbishop Rivera y Damas with both the Salvadoran military and the opposition forces. In response to the strong desire of an increasing number of displaced persons within El Salvador to return to their original towns and to rebuild them, CRIPDES (Christian Committee of the Displaced of El Salvador) formed a program committee, the CNR (National Coordinating Committee for Repopulation) in May 1986, and within that year successfully assisted in the repopulation of two other towns, San Jose las Flores in Chalatenango and El Barillo in Cuscatlan. In both instances, delegations of North American religious persons, coordinated by the Interfaith Office on Accompaniment, accompanied the *repobladores*, returning to the US with inspiring accounts of the courage of these people (Dahlberg 4).

News of these initial successes motivated the refugees of Mesa Grande to begin to organize themselves to return en masse to their own villages, which were little more than bombed-out ruins. Meanwhile, a more positive international climate was developing in Central America among the presidents of the five countries. The signing of Esquipulas II in August 1987 was particularly encouraging, as among other things it recognized the refugees' legal right to return to their towns of origin. Thus, the refugees in Honduras built upon their own hard-won successes in the camps, upon the growing movement toward repopulation within their country, and upon the international support developing for this movement from various quarters. With these foundations, they chose to re-enter El Salvador, to reclaim their homes, and to work nonviolently to create peace. They hoped their efforts would continue to be monitored by an ongoing presence of international delegations.

Eager to see the refugees leave Honduras, the Honduran government had joined with the UNHCR and the Salvadoran government in a Tripartite Commission. After Esquipulas II and CNR's success in 1986 with indigenous repopulations, the refugees of Mesa Grande gained some leverage and began to demonstrate their ability to negotiate terms for repatriation. The refugees' platforms for repatriation included: (a) that the Salvadoran government and their armed forces not impede people from churches and humanitarian groups, both Salvadoran and foreign, who wished to accompany the refugees from the camps to the repopulated communities; (b) that the refugees be given safe passage to the repopulation sites (their original villages) without interrogations, searches, or psychological pressures; (c) that official status be given to a mediation commission of high-level Salvadoran church officials; (d) that the government's armed and guerrilla forces cease all military operations between the dates of the departure from the camps and their arrival; (f) that the refugees be allowed to carry with them their basic materials from the camp, including food, medicine, tools, construction materials, clothing, agricultural supplies, etc.; and (g) that the government respect the status of civilians and end military operations against repopulated communities. The *directivas* spent many arduous months ironing out these terms among the refugees and subsequently with the Tripartite Commission.

The decision to return was both a community and an individual family decision, one in which people knew that they were taking the ultimate risk of their lives by returning to the very areas where armed conflict was still raging. There were extensive preparations to be made for moving such large numbers of people and their possessions from the camps as well. People decided at different times that they were ready to go, each time learning from the successes or difficulties of previous returns.

Throughout this period the refugees endured continual struggles with the UNHCR and the Salvadoran government, which necessitated long delays. The refugees, however, would not be deterred from their goals, and by October 1987, the first historic group from Mesa Grande left in a massive, well-organized, and celebrative caravan to repopulate such villages as Santa Marta, Copapayo, Las Vueltas, Guarjila, and San Antonio los Ranchos. This first repatriation would be followed by two other large groups in the fall of 1988, and the fourth *retorno* in October 1989, by far the most difficult as it came when the new Cristiani government had been in power for only a few months. A total of over 8,000 refugees

returned in these four caravans, along with about 1,000 who returned on an individual basis. Only around 2,000 refugees remained in Mesa Grande by early 1990.

In Colomoncagua carefully developed plans for repatriation in the fall of 1989 were made more difficult by the extreme escalation of the war between the FMLN and the armed forces, particularly in San Salvador and other urban areas. Along with the persecution of Salvadoran church leaders, including key members of CNR, the Salvadoran government withdrew its earlier agreements to support the repatriation movement. Likewise, the UNHCR reneged and refused to provide the essential vehicles for transport of some of the Colomoncagua groups. Through great ingenuity and determination, however, the Colomoncagua *directiva* proceeded with its plans and convinced the Honduran government at least to cooperate. Later the UNHCR rejoined the negotiations and persuaded the Salvadoran government to do likewise. Therefore, between November 1989 and February 27, 1990, 8,400 refugees from Colomoncagua returned to Meanguera, Morazan, in successive waves, creating a town which they named in honor of the recently martyred Jesuit, Segundo Montes. By March 3, 1990, the 1,300 refugees of the San Antonio camp successfully returned en masse, settling in Gualcho, Usulutan.

In a very short time, each of the highly organized caravans from both Mesa Grande and Colomoncagua has become legend, and the book which follows chronicles some of the great adversities and triumphs the refugees experienced in these consecutive returns to their country.

In the repopulated towns, the newly repatriated citizens are integrating their ancient agricultural traditions with their newly acquired skills, creating a broad range of health and education services and productive workshops. They continue their training programs from the camps. Best of all, they are raising their children outside of a prison environment and upon their native soil.

In the three years that have followed since the first caravan left Mesa Grande, one can only marvel at the reports which have come from international visitors about the cluster of repopulated towns and communities, now over 30, in the northern and eastern provinces. You will read some of these reports. You will hear the former refugees (now sometimes called the *repobladores*) tell their epic story of exile and peacemaking. You will encounter insightful and stirring narratives of accompaniment.

The reader will find the many contributions by Salvadorans and by internationals (primarily North Americans) to be varied in format, including direct interviews, descriptive vignettes about the people, travel notes, letters from the refugees and from others, journals, essays, songs, and outstanding photography. The material is organized thematically around life before and in the camps, the going home experience itself, life in the villages, and the meaning of accompaniment.

It is important to note that pseudonyms have been used for all of the refugees who are mentioned, described, or quoted in these pages. Photographs have been selected which are thematically relevant to the text, but they do not depict actual persons or places described in the text, unless so indicated. These precautions have been taken at the recommendation of the human rights organizations.

The Project Committee would like to express deep appreciation to all of the persons who have so graciously shared their materials and ideas, and those who have given us other forms of support, including financial backing. Particularly, the Committee would like to express gratitude to the Going Home Campaign, the SHARE Foundation, and the Interfaith Office on Accompaniment for their direct consultation and encouragement.

It is our sincere hope that this volume will provide new information and insights concerning the repatriation and repopulation movements in El Salvador and thereby increase recognition and support for the courageous and very talented former refugees who have so richly inspired all of those who have met them.

V.C., Spring 1990

WORKS CITED

Amnesty International. Submission to the Inter-American Commission on Human Rights of the Organization of American States. March 21, 1980.

Berryman, Phillip. *Notes on El Salvador: Deepening Crisis— Prospects for Peace?* Philadelphia: NARMIC/American Friends Sevice Commission, 1989.

Carmada, Renato. *Forced to Move.* San Francisco: Solidarity Publications, 1985.

Dahlberg, Lana and José Escobar. "A Call to Accompaniment: American Religious Response to Repopulation in El Salvador." San Francisco: Justice and Peace Commission of the Archdiocese of San Francisco, Central American Refugee Organizing Project of Catholic Social Services, the SHARE Foundation, September 1986. (Available through the Interfaith Office on Accompaniment, 1050 S. Vaness Avenue, San Francisco, California 94110.)

A Dream Compels Us: The Voices of Salvadoran Women, edited by B. Carter, K. Insko, D. Loeb, and M. Tobias. Boston: South End Press, 1989.

"Salvadoran Refugees in Honduras: Honduranization and Repatriation, Parts of the Counterinsurgency Plan." Managua, Nicaragua: PROCARES, 1987.

Schmidt, Arthur. "Salvadoran Refugees at Colomoncagua Seek to Return to Their Zone of Origin in El Salvador." Philadelphia: Department of History, Temple University, 1989. Unpublished manuscript.

PART I

LIFE BEFORE AND IN THE CAMPS

JOHN GRANT: *Mother and daughter, San Jose las Flores, December 1987.*

Chapter 1

"WE WILL DANCE, AND GO SWIMMING IN THE RIVER" STORIES OF THE PEOPLE

In this chapter you will encounter portraits of *campesinos* who were so severely attacked by the Salvadoran army in the late 1970s and early 1980s that they could no longer remain on their land. They made their way to the refugee camps in Honduras, often losing family members in the massacres that plagued their flight. You meet them as they reflect on their past and plan to return to their homelands in El Salvador seven to nine years later.

These people are survivors. Many of them lost children, spouses, and elderly parents in the tragic pre-flight and flight violence, but they still believe in the future.

You will meet them through direct interviews as well as through the eyes and ears of North Americans who visited the camps and, in many cases, accompanied the refugees on their journey home. The nuns, priests, social workers, housewives, teachers, and retirees who recorded these stories did so in an attitude of love and admiration, but it was the refugees themselves who inspired such respect.

Colomoncagua, Honduras, December 1989

"I WAS THE ONLY ONE THAT I EVER FOUND THAT HAD SURVIVED FROM OUR TOWN" (An Interview with María on the Mozote Massacre)

I am María. I was born in the village of Mozote Meanguera. That was my place, the place of the great massacre on the 11th of December 1981, when a great number of the army came.

The army came in the afternoon. They told everyone to come into the street and lie down on their faces. They searched everyone and took whatever money or jewelry people had. Even the children had to lie down on the street with us. At about 7:00 at night they had everyone get up. They stuck us in houses and told us that we shouldn't even stick our noses out of the doors or they would shoot us.

At 5:00 in the morning on the 11th, they started taking us out of the houses and lined us up in the street in front of the church. They had a line of women and a line of men, and at the heads of the lines they had soldiers facing us. From 5:00 in the morning we were there. The children were hungry and it was cold; they kept crying.

By 7:00 in the morning, the helicopters came. They landed in the center of the market area throwing up dust. A lot of military people were there. Perhaps the helicopter brought the order to kill everyone because that's when they started to blindfold the men and throw them face down on the ground, and that's when people began screaming and yelling. Women and children were herded into the church. There was one window where people were able to climb up and look out of the church and see what was happening to the men. That's when the soldiers came with knives and guns and started threatening us—putting knives to the children and poking and hitting us with the rifles.

I had a child at my breast. I was standing looking out the window, and I could see that they were beginning to kill the men. I told the other women, and we started screaming, "Don't kill them! Don't kill them!"

By about noon, they had killed all the men, and the soldiers were coming in to take the young girls to the hillside to rape them. They were taking the young girls away from their mothers and beating the mothers as they took their children away. Then they started to take the older women and the women who were crying; there were even deaf and dumb people who were taken out. Finally they took the children, even the children who were two days old—and pregnant women. We could see that they were starting to sharpen their knives and that they were making fuses for starting fires.

At that point, a group of 22 women, leaving our children behind (I left four children), went to the house where they were killing people. We could see that the house was filled with dead people. We screamed together, "Don't kill them! Don't kill them! Leave them alone!" And the soldiers said, "Well, the devil will come to take them away. Don't cry." And some young girls who were sick were clinging to their mothers and crying, "Don't kill them!"

At that point, I knelt down by a soldier and begged him, and I prayed to God to save me, because I had nothing else left to do except to pray to God. And then I was able to get behind the soldier and hide behind a tree. At that point, the soldiers were distracted by the people crying, and they didn't see where I was. I was hiding practically at the feet of a soldier. I hid myself behind a branch so that only my feet were sticking out. Quickly I covered my feet so the soldier would not see, and he killed all the other women I was with.

At 6:00 in the afternoon, they were finished with killing the women; only a few children were left. I heard one soldier say, "What shall we do with the children who are left over? They'll end up dying anyway because they don't have anybody left to take care of them. We should kill them because otherwise they will all become guerrillas." Another soldier said, "I don't want to kill that many children." (There were a lot of beautiful children.) "We could take them." And the first soldier said, "The order from the colonel is that we kill them all, and that we should kill everyone in Mozote and everyone in this zone. All the people in this area should be killed. What we should do now is set fire to the house. That way we will take care of everyone."

So at night they set fire to the house. The fire was so close to me that the leaves on the tree I was hiding behind began

RENATO CARMADA: *A mother attempts to identify her daugher's skull among those found in a well full of death squad victims.*

to catch fire. I was waiting to see if anyone came out of the fire, but no one came out. There was still one child crying, and the soldier shot. I heard the shot! He shot the last child while I was hiding practically in the street behind this tree.

Eventually they left three soldiers to watch the fire in the building; the rest went to the store. The soldiers left by the burning house fell asleep, so I gradually began to think about escaping. I saw some cattle and some dogs come down the street, escaping from the fire, and then I could see how to escape, how to find my way out of the street and into the fields. My dress was a white dress; I covered it with mud so that I could blend in with the animals and perhaps look like an animal as I escaped.

I lay down in the field with the animals, and I began to cry, to pray crying for my children, because I had been there, and I could still hear the cries of the children, calling, "Mamma! Mamma!" I could still hear the noise when the soldiers cut the throats of the children. So I prayed to the Lord to give me a very strong spirit, and I prayed that he would give me the strength not to go back, so that I could go further away and not keep hearing the voices of the children.

I pulled myself on the ground, crawling away from the soldiers. I kept going further down the hill. Then somebody saw me and started shooting, and I hid behind a cactus. Eventually they went back up to the village. I kept hearing their voices, but they didn't find me.

The next day at 6:00 in the morning, I could hear that they were killing the young girls. (I had heard the cries of the young girls from the hillside all night.) The helicopter came again. I went a little closer to see it land near Mozote. After it took off, bombs dropped from the sky big enough to blow up an animal. I heard shooting from the surrounding villages. By 3:00 in the afternoon, I was seeing smoke coming from those other places as if those people were being burned too. By 5:00 in the afternoon, I could tell they were burning the pigs and the trees as well. So again I went back to praying, and then I ran away.

I ran through a sugarcane field to a farm at the edge of a sort of gully. I hid in the bottom of the gully and crawled on my hands and knees until I found a little house at the edge of the river. I hid around a corner of the house. I didn't want to go inside, because I was afraid people might come and find me there. I spent about four days there. This was about six days that I had not had anything to eat. Finally I found an old jug in the house and went to the river to get water.

At the river I saw two children. I was so happy to see that there was someone else alive. I followed the road where these children had come from, and one child said to her mother, "Look, here comes María." The mother ran toward me, "María, Here you are!" She asked me about my family. I said, "All I can tell you is they've all been killed, and I cannot say anything more." I couldn't say anything more because I was crying too much. So she embraced me and said, "Well, come with us."

She took us (me and the two children), and we fled together. We didn't take corn or anything. We just went as fast as we could to hide in a cave where others were hiding. There was another woman that I knew in the cave; she told

PAUL SCIRE: *Mesa Grande, 1987.*

me what had been happening the four days that I had been hiding out and weeping. Finally I got something to eat; she gave me sugarcane which was the first food I had had in several days.

A year later we came here (1982) . . . . We could see that this was an organized community that worked and lived collectively. They shared their food and their cooking, so when we came, people came forward to welcome us and give us food. We joined this community and lived in community, and we have learned about unity. Working together in the vegetable growing and in the cooking and in the workshops is a better way. . . . We can participate in health care and share things with each other, even our sufferings and our Bible study. We share our faith, our worries, and our concern about what has happened in El Salvador. . . .

Now we want to go back and hope we can contribute what we have been through and what we have learned. We are looking for peace and justice for our country and hope that the children who have survived will have a better life. We hope that we will not live the way we did before—separately—but that we'll be unified and that people will respect our lives.

Lempira, Honduras, March 1981

"A BAPTISM OF FIRE"
(The Lempa River Massacre)

The waters of the Rio Lempa divide the dry hills of Lempira, Honduras, from Cabañas, El Salvador; waters no wider than a stone's throw across to the other shore and just deep enough to reach over the head of a man or woman. On both sides of the river the hills rise sharply to a crest; cliffs and trees jut out into the water to offer protection from the sun . . . .

Wednesday, March 18th. Today, at the Rio Lempa, 4,000 refugees crossed over. In the darkness of the dawn hours, they began to cross, cautiously. Now the hills are filled with men, women, and children—above all, children. Cries fill the air. Men and women in the river pass children over their shoulders to the other side. Everywhere shouts, mortar fire on both sides of the river. Then in the sky, a helicopter. Shots of machine-gun fire and several sweeps over the river. Unmistakable signs of a Salvadoran helicopter and the Security forces. Rush to safety behind the cliffs and trees, then back to the river. Hundreds crossing. Everywhere cries fill the air. A baptism by fire . . . .

Two days later we decided to return to the river to investigate, to look for survivors. To return, just to return. Something happened here which we still cannot believe. The return is more difficult. By now the Honduran soldiers have mobilized. We are checked every hundred yards along the way—negotiating, displaying passports, bags and possessions searched. We travel as a "commission," as journalists, and are able to pass. At the last checkpoint, the soldiers inform us that they are prohibited to go any further, and we travel at our own risk.

We approach the river with great anticipation. What will we encounter? And who? The dead? The missing? Those who have managed to cross the river and who have saved themselves?

Along the way we see unmistakable signs of the battle the day before; rocks piled up in circles like miniature caves behind which the people hid from the helicopter fire. Huge holes gape in the ground where the mortar fell. On Honduran territory! There is no mistake. I reach down and pick up the lead fragments of the mortar. This is the neutrality; this is the peace which falls from the lips of the generals and politicians.

Suddenly someone shouts out ahead: "We've found somebody! He's alive!" As we approach, we find an old man; the gray in his hair and the features on his face show 80 or 90 years of age. He can hardly speak for fear and exhaustion. He lies still by the tree. Someone from his village recognizes him. "That's Don Felipe!"

A little further toward the river we encounter more refugees: three women and their children. What joy! A little further on we find a small child, four years, old, lying still on the rocks. Her mother brings us closer and turns the child over. She cries out in pain. Half of her backside is torn away, infested with flies and dirt. Her mother informs us it was a helicopter which did it. *"Animales"* the people say to refer to helicopters and planes.

At last we reach the river and climb down the steep cliffs to the water. "Here's another! Dead." There stretched out on the rocks is a woman, 60 years old. Her mouth is open and turned toward the sky: silence. Her hands, folded across her chest, are clutching a straw cross. Her clothes are soaked in blood. No one speaks. Only the water ebbs on the shore.

"Salvador!" another man who is with us cries out to the other shore. "Salvador!" He is looking for his ten-year-old son who did not cross over. We have to restrain him to prevent him from [entering the river]. "Salvador!" he cries again. "Salvador!"

The return home is somber. Exhaustion and the heat of the day subdue us. Over our shoulders we carry the old man and the little girl in hammocks. The soldiers stop and search us and let us pass. At one stop, I call out for water for the little girl. No one responds. Then a soldier steps up and offers some water from his canteen. The little girl drinks thirstily. The soldier, no more than 20, looks like so many of the peasants here. The woman next to me urges me to drink too. I am unable to.

Finally we arrive at the camp. A makeshift clinic has been set up to attend to the refugees. Someone attends to the little girl. The old man rests in the shade. Next to me a mother feeds her child through a medicine dropper. On a cot another child receives nourishment intravenously. His belly is extended, his ribs pronounced, his eyes stare out into the distance. I reach out to touch his forehead. By morning both children are dead.

S.W.

STEVE CAGAN: *Salvadoran refugees, Mesa Grande refugee camp, Honduras, August 1982.*

Mesa Grande, Honduras, October 1989

"WHEN YOU VISIT ME IN EL SALVADOR, WE WILL DANCE, AND GO SWIMMING IN THE RIVER"

One of the most memorable people I met in Mesa Grande, whose face I hold in my heart, is Ruth. She is one of the few women on the *directivas* and a single mother with three children. When we came to the meeting of her *directiva*, she seemed rather quiet, and when she stood up to introduce herself, we thought she said, "I'm sorry that I'm just a woman." But that didn't seem to hold her back.

At the end of the meeting, one of our delegation members asked for quotes for the press, and she said: "Due to the nature of the present government in El Salvador, you may be aware of the lack of human rights in our country. To confront this, the people unite to get them back. So the government will try to stop them, to capture and kill them. I want to ask all of you. . . to denounce that, as the government will be afraid of you."

She was so animated, so alive—I think a couple of us fell in love with her. She brought me into her home, apologizing for her one-room house and explaining that "only four people live here." She was aware of what her community

LAURA JACKSON: *Salvadoran refugee, Honduras, December 1989.*

faced going back, but saw no other alternative than organizing for the strength to stand up for their most basic rights: freedom to live in peace, to work, to feed the children. When I asked her what it was going to be like for her children to leave the camp, she said she was going to show them "a whole new world."

As I left, Ruth gave me a big hug and promised me, "When you visit me in El Salvador, we will dance, and go swimming in the river." I sure hope I can.

E.F.

Colomoncagua, Honduras, December 1989

"THE WHOLE COMMUNITY CAME OUT AND DEMONSTRATED" (Interview with Elisa)

My name is Elisa. I am 52 years old, and I came here to the refugee camp in 1981, and so I am here nine years as a refugee.... When I first came here I worked in education in 1982 and 1983. Then I worked in other areas, with the group of mothers and in pastoral work. Lately we are trying to improve our level of organization. And so around the middle of 1988, the different committees were formed—health, education, pastoral work, the mothers—and that is when I switched to the Reception Committee. Our work is to receive our brothers and sisters who come to visit us from all over the world to get to know our situation. So we receive them; we have a welcoming ceremony and then we plan their visit according to the interests they have, whether it is in health, education, etc. I think it is an important work....

In the last months of 1987 and the beginning of 1988, there was a great deal of repression. The military was patrolling in the camps three times a day. And there were Salvadoran soldiers as well as Honduran soldiers. They had their faces painted and threatened the people; they put the point of the knife up to the face of a child. And the whole community came out and demonstrated because we didn't think it was right that they should beat up a child or an old person. They even shot off rounds inside the camps.

This repression culminated with the death of Mr. Pedro Lopez, 63 years old. He was working in the farm at Copinol. That day, the 23rd of April, at 9:00 in the morning, we heard four shots. And it was at that moment that he was assassinated. After that, the community got together, and when the lieutenant came later to acknowledge the death, we weren't afraid; rather we felt strength. We didn't want him to come in to see the body; we wouldn't let him close to the body. Later a truck full of soldiers came into the camp. But we felt a deep pain in our consciences, and so the entire community came out into the street and had a demonstration,

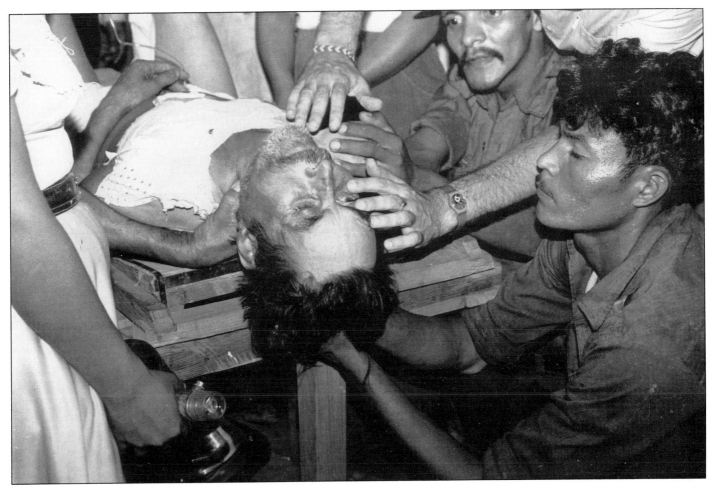

DODY RIGGS: *Pedro Lopez attended by family and friends.*

repudiating this assassination. We weren't in agreement that the soldiers should drive through our camps. The trucks that belonged to the agencies that worked in our community weren't to be used hauling soldiers. We made the soldiers get out and walk out of the camp. Since then, the military have not entered the camps. We can't say that there is no more oppression, however, because they are still all around the camps, and they capture people sometimes, old people and children.

Mesa Grande, Honduras, October 1989

"LANGUAGE WAS NO BARRIER AS WE EMBRACED"

As I was returning from the assembly called by the Salvadoran leaders, an elderly lady invited me into her home to show me preparations that had been made for their departure. Her household things were packed on one side. Seeing a cat, I asked her if the cat would also go. She smiled and assured me that it would. She then led me outside, reached into a large kettle on the roof and gave me a tamale—food apparently prepared for the journey. Language was no barrier as we embraced. Her quiet serenity, her joy, and her courage will not soon be erased from my memory.

E.L.

Mesa Grande, Honduras, October 1988

"MIGUEL . . . WAS THE EMBODIMENT OF THE COLLECTIVE JOY AND HOPE OF THE REFUGEE COMMUNITY"

Perhaps the most impressive person I encountered during our stay at Mesa Grande was the first person who spoke to me. A wiry man of approximately my age sidled up to me, and in a friendly, confident voice said, *"Alegre, mi amigo, alegre."* ("Be happy, my friend, be happy.") These were the words that initiated a transformation of my images of "refugees" and what they are supposed to be like. Here I had traveled a thousand miles to "accompany" and lend assistance to a people in need, when suddenly I found myself on the receiving end of words of comfort in a curious role reversal. [This delegation had struggled for 48 hours to obtain permission to enter the camp.]

Miguel, the man who spoke then, gently patted my shoulder, and then extended his hand in greeting. He had angular features, a mop of curly brown hair, a slender build, and the kind of rough hands that could handle the business end of a machete for hours in a new corn field.

The affinity which I felt with Miguel grew rapidly as I recognized in him a reflection of much of the pain of the Sal-

ADAM KUFELD: *Santa Marta.*

RICK REINHARD: *Campesino with son.*

JOHN GRANT: *Napping baby, San Jose las Flores, March 1989.*

vadoran people, especially that of the refugees who have been so violently uprooted from their homelands in Cuscatlan. During the brief time which we shared, Miguel revealed that he had lost both his wife and infant child during their flight from the murderous insanity of both Salvadoran and Honduran armies who fired at them as they attempted to swim across the river border.

The *"alegre"* of which Miguel spoke emerged from another side of his character. He was also the embodiment of the collective joy and hope of the refugee community as they prepared for the fourth repatriation. Not only was he firmly committed to returning to his home community, he felt profoundly responsible for the refugee community at Mesa Grande. This was revealed by the fact that he had postponed his repatriation on previous occasions in order to maintain continuity of leadership within the camps. Other people spoke very highly of his dedication to the task of "conscienticizing" community members who were still hesitant to support the planned move. Here was a prime example of the developing collective consciousness of the community which was opening up new horizons beyond immediate personal interests.

Just before we departed from Mesa Grande, Miguel and his youthful new wife Eva, a leader in her own right, revealed that they were expecting their first child in a matter of months. They expressed a deep hope that their child would be born in El Salvador. How obvious the symbolism would be! A new life in a new family making a fresh start with the hope of peace and justice in a new El Salvador!

N.V.

Colomoncagua, Honduras, December 1989

"WE DON'T KNOW ANYTHING OF THEM" (An Interview with Amparo)

My name is Amparo. My son and another boy disappeared the 3rd of November. At about 3:00 in the afternoon, Carlos and Toño went to bathe. And from the 3rd of November up until now we don't know anything of them. . . .

We are very worried. These boys spent all their time working in the factory (workshop). They didn't go out and wander around. Something could happen to someone who was wandering around carelessly out there. But these boys were always around the camps, with us . . . .

On other occasions kids have been captured and tortured but then given back, but this time it seems very bad. And what worries us most is that now we are on the eve of returning to our country. If we leave Honduras, then they could be left here, isolated. . . . What shall we do? We can't just leave them here. They are the hope that we have, that one day they will care for us, working. This was our only boy . . . .

LAURA JACKSON: *Two young boys from Colomoncagua.*

Mesa Grande, Honduras, October 1989

"LIGHT SHONE FROM HIS FACE. . . OF DIGNITY, OF HOPE, OF INCREDIBLE FAITH"

I met Orlando at the first meeting we had with *directiva* members. After the meeting was over, I noticed him walking around chewing on a piece of sugarcane. I was curious about this as I'd seen many of the folks in the camp eating it. So I asked him where he got it, and he informed me that they grew it! I hadn't been aware that they cultivated crops in the camp, so I asked him to show me where. He took me to the edge of the mesa and indicated the hillsides sloping down all around the camp; there he pointed out the crops of corn, banana trees, mango trees, and sugarcane. The refugees had planted them soon after they arrived in Mesa Grande, and the crops were doing well. "Of course," I said, "You are farmers!"

"Yes, but we are not only farmers," he answered. "Since

we have been here, we have learned how to read and write, how to fix machines and make shoes. And when we go back, we will be even more self-sufficient than before."

Then he started telling me about the trip back, how excited he was, how beautiful the caravan would be with music playing and banners. "We are going home to live in peace and justice," he said. "And I know you know this, because you are helping us. Although there are many obstacles, they won't stop us. *Cuando vamos, nos vamos!*" ("When we go, we're going to go!")

Well, the whole time he was talking to me—and, mind you, he hadn't prepared a speech—this light shone from his face. It was the light of dignity, of hope, of incredible faith in his own and his community's ability to rebuild their lives in the midst of real evil and oppression.

E.F.

STEVE CAGAN

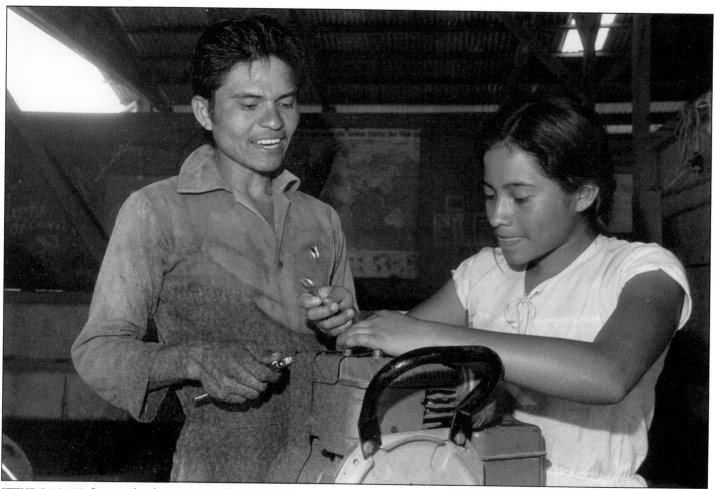

STEVE CAGAN: *Instruction in a camp machine workshop.*

Chapter 2

"THERE ARE REALLY COLORS EVERYWHERE"
ORGANIZING DYNAMIC OF THE PEOPLE
IN A REPRESSIVE POLITICAL CLIMATE

As you will see in the following pages, almost everyone who has visited the refugee camps in Honduras has had two similar responses. First there is dismay at the dreary living conditions forced upon these people, conditions more suggestive of a penal camp than of a place of safe refuge. Their lives are encased in barbed wire or military cordons; they are cut off from Honduran markets and social events; they are not given sufficient land to feed themselves; their houses are crowded together, and they are continually subjected to army surveillance and searches. Members of the community have been detained, tortured, and "disappeared" by the Honduran military. In addition to these tangible evidences of deprivation, refugees tell of continual attempts on the part of the United Nations High Commission on Refugees as well as the Salvadoran government to control their present and future lives. Like persons in penal camps, they have been told in many subtle and unsubtle ways how very insignificant they are.

The second response, however, is admiration at how splendidly the refugees have organized their lives in the camps, how tenaciously they have held on to their dignity and their insistence that they *will* be a vital part of the negotiations that determine their future. They have learned new production skills from various relief agency workers and then taught them to each other; they have worked out a system of governance that takes cognizance of the basic needs of all members of the community; they have reversed inefficient and psychologically damaging aspects of *machis-*

STEVE CAGAN: *Mesa Grande, 1982.*

mo culture. Cut off from the world, they have built a world for themselves, one that could well model the kind of democratic cooperation necessary for the creation of a new and just El Salvador.

Mesa Grande, Honduras, October 1989

"THOUGH AT FIRST GLANCE THE CAMP SEEMS GREY AND BROWN, THERE ARE REALLY COLORS EVERYWHERE"

The approach to the Mesa Grande camp is guarded by Honduran military personnel—mainly teenage boys carrying large guns. Once we surrendered our passports, secure that we would leave the camp promptly at 5:00 p.m., we were allowed past the simple wooden gate that the refugees are not permitted to go near on pain of death.

The first impression of the camp is bleak. Mesa Grande looks like it was hacked out of the surrounding hills, which are green and lovely. The camp, in contrast, is a flat, dusty plain—or a muddy one when the daily rain falls. The buildings look as though they were slapped up in a hurry, then left to disintegrate slowly. Originally set up as temporary housing for 2,000, Mesa Grande has held over 12,000 and the wear and tear shows. The houses are wood and corrugated-iron shacks that are drafty and patched with trash. There are rows of tin latrines at intervals, and open-air cinderblock showers and laundry areas. The whole camp is encircled with barbed wire, making it seem more like a prison than a refuge for war survivors.

But despite the bleakness, the camp generates an overwhelming feeling of hope. On all of the hillsides, sloping away from the camp, are crops the refugees have cultivated since they first arrived. There are also workshops where the refugees make their own clothing and shoes and repair tractors and other mechanical equipment. Though at first glance, the camp seems grey and brown, there are really colors everywhere, in the flapping quilts on clotheslines, strung all along the perimeter of the camp and across some of the small alleys, and in the bright clothes of the women and girls.

The buildings themselves attest to the refugees' determination; graffiti has been sprayed in many places. The messages say such things as "to return is our right; our country awaits us" and "hooray for the fourth return." There are also entreaties to the soldiers who guard them to stop hurting the defenseless people, and to the UN High Commission on Refugees—the supervisor of the camp—to restore the badly needed medical care. On one building, above a mural depicting the repatriation with buses travelling along blue roads across green hills, is the message: "To return is our right. We ask the military and the government to respect our dignity."

E.F.

STEVE CAGAN: *Cooperatively run gardens in a refugee camp.*

HARVEY FINKLE: *Mesa Grande, 1987.*

ADAM KUFELD: *At the camp's distribution center, a girl receives produce for her family.*

Colomoncagua, Honduras, December 1989

"WE NEEDED TO WORK IN COLLECTIVES BECAUSE THERE WEREN'T ENOUGH KITCHEN UTENSILS FOR EACH FAMILY" (Interview with the *Directiva*)

When we first arrived here, we realized that there had to be a coordinator to administer the few goods that were arriving for the community. . . . Then we saw we needed to put up buildings, housing. So we needed a coordinator for this work, also for the work of agriculture and for the kitchen. That's when we saw we needed to work in collectives, because there weren't enough kitchen utensils for each family to make their food individually.

In 1983 we began the workshops. And so with each work area that opened, we looked for a coordinator. Each year we have modified a little, always looking for the best way to administer the goods of our community. Last year, in 1988, we had a very important experience when we held the Fast Against Hunger and Repression. During the fast, it wasn't the coordinators of each sub-camp that coordinated and discussed issues, but rather the coordinators of each of the work places. . . .

Each sub-camp is divided into colonies; one camp may

have ten colonies, another seven, etc. And in each colony there are around 120 to 130 people. So now each colony names one person to be responsible for the nutrition of their 120 people. It is this person's responsibility to oversee a just distribution of food. The same is true for health. There is one person to watch over the health of 120 people. And so it goes. There is one person to see to the distribution of clothes, shoes, housing, etc. There is someone who looks after all the needs of the colony—the environment, social problems, pastoral needs, education. Everything begins in the colony.

Colomoncagua, Honduras, December 1989

"THE BEGINNING IS WITH CHILDREN" (Interview with Ligeia)

My name is Ligeia, and I am 18 years old. In 1981 work in education was begun, not very formal, not detailed, because we didn't have many possibilities, no materials or personnel to help us. But there were a few people who knew how to read and write and they started with the children, because the beginning is with the children. And since we didn't have any materials, we began by giving pieces of cardboard to the children and charcoal so they could write. Then, with the years, people from other countries began to come here to help us. They were able to bring a few materials, and so we began to give pieces of paper to the children, not notebooks, but pieces of paper. We progressed from there.

An idea of ours was to teach how we came here, why we came from El Salvador. This is what we taught first, and the little bit that we knew. It was here that I learned. With the years, we also began workshops so that the children could learn to work. Besides the classes, they would learn other work. Later, adults were incorporated into the classes.

The first work the children learned was in a workshop we call "manual things" (where they learn to use their hands, for example, in embroidery). The community feels it is necessary for the children to learn work from the time they are little—whatever chores or work that we do here in the camps—because before we didn't know how to do any of the things we are doing here. We were peasants; we didn't know how to do any of these things. And so we thought that here we should teach the children from the time they are little, because when we go back to our country, it will be a great asset for us.

STEVE CAGAN: *A young adult provides instruction in writing at a camp school.*

STEVE CAGAN: *Salvadoran refugees, Mesa Grande refugee camp, Honduras, August 1982.*

Mesa Grande, Honduras, August 1988

"I WAS CONSTANTLY AMAZED AT THE STRENGTH OF THEIR ORGANIZATION"

In the three days we were at Mesa Grande, I saw only one toy that had been produced outside the camp—a plastic doll, naked and minus one leg. However, there was no shortage of toys. Balls made from string, small stones somewhat round used as marbles for the boys and jacks for the girls. A teeter-totter was fashioned out of a log and a rough board. In some ways there was no need for dolls; every little girl at some point in the day was actually caring for her baby sister or brother. I will never forget the sight of those little ones, some in flip-flops, some in tennis shoes, many walking barefoot on the rocky road—ever present and welcomed in any setting, learning by watching and listening.

I was constantly amazed at the strength of the refugees' organization and their ability to make decisions by consensus. We were told that the refugees had set up a structure for communication so that every person in the camp of some 6,500 refugees could be contacted within 10 to 20 minutes. I know it to be true, because we witnessed several examples through the time of negotiation preceding and during the repatriation. These people had banded together in an incredible way for survival. There was no room in their situation for petty disagreements. Standing in solidarity was crucial and, because of their common focus, easily attainable.

M.L.M.

Colomoncagua, Honduras, December 1989

"IT WAS THE REFUGEES THEMSELVES WHO DECIDED WHAT THEY WANTED AND WHAT THEY DID NOT WANT"

While in other parts of the world refugees often assume an attitude of dependency and passive acceptance of help, in the Salvadoran camps it was the refugees themselves who decided what they wanted and what they did not want, participating directly in the organization of the camps. The reasons for such a difference are not difficult to understand: these were people who in their own homeland had fought hard for their rights, who knew their rights, and were not willing to let anybody else control their lives.

Thus began the struggle of the refugees to maintain and

STEVE CAGAN: *Mesa Grande, 1982.*

STEVE CAGAN: *Work in the carpentry and tailoring workshops.*

develop their own identity. The Honduras army, allied de facto to the Salvadoran army, maintained a military *cordon sanitaire* around the camps through those nine years of exile. Hundreds of human rights violations were committed by these soldiers; dozens of refugees were killed or made to disappear. In truth, the military presence transformed the refugee camps into gigantic jails.

But within these jails unusual things have happened. For one thing, although the refugees recognize the role of the UNHCR in terms of their providing protection and safety, they have never been willing to accept the paternalistic, often antagonistic, attitude of the UNHCR toward them.

In other words, the community has organized itself and become able to produce a great quantity of the goods necessary for its day-to-day survival, remaining independent of outside economic forces due to its complete separation from the outside market world. The Honduran government was completely opposed to any type of integration of the refugees into the local environment. It thus happened that a peasant refugee community used the time they had to spend in exile as a means to step out of the ignorance and isolation traditionally imposed upon them and to learn new skills that would eventually allow them to return to their country with extremely useful knowledge.

In this process, furthermore, the traditional oppressive sex roles suffered a transformation. Women were a majority in the camps and were forced to assume many of the jobs traditionally assigned to men. "When I arrived here," says María, 42, "all I knew was how to make children and tortil-las. Now I have worked as a teacher, a nurse, and have been camp organizer for six years."

R.C.

Colomoncagua, Honduras, December 1989

"WOMEN HAVE JUST ABOUT THE SAME CAPACITY AS MEN" (Interview with Elisa)

Before coming here, we women, maybe not just me—our work was to live in the house, cooking, working, and having children. We never had the opportunity to go to a workshop or do some other work. Most of the men are peasants. And so the work of the women was to grind corn, bring the firewood, feed the workers, and take them their lunch in the fields. That was my work. We can also say that we women were shy and timid. Besides being afraid of our husbands, we were afraid to talk. It was fear, since we have never had participation like we do here. For us all of these rights were denied. Now we can say that the life we are taking back to El Salvador is very different. . . .

STEVE CAGAN: *A woman gives instruction in business administration.*

Everything that we have learned here in exile, we want to share. The idea that men and women can develop. We would say that women have just about the same capacity as men to develop themselves in the form that they want to, and also in work. Here you will see that there is not a single type of work that women don't do.

In El Salvador, a woman couldn't go off to work, far away, because her husband might worry if she was working with another man. He might wonder what work they were doing! Now that doesn't happen here. Here men work in one place, women in another; men may work with different women, and women with different men. There is no problem.

Mesa Grande, Honduras, October 1989

"THERE WAS ALWAYS MUSIC— FREE SONGS ON THE GUITAR AND SINGING"

Preparations to leave were well under way when we arrived in the camp on October 15th. On the 16th we were taken

LAURA JACKSON: *Girls playing soccer in Colomoncagua.*

RENATO CARMADA: *Songs describing the struggles and victories of refugee life are composed and performed, mostly by youths in the camps. The instruments are often handcrafted in camp workshops.*

on a tour of the camps to meet the people. A group of women were grinding and washing corn, some were packing, and some were cooking food for the journey. The men were taking down the houses and stacking and binding materials to be picked up by the trucks. The children were also working—some of the smaller ones were tending the toddlers. All of the people worked together. It was real teamwork.

There was a man who had gone blind since he had come to Mesa Grande. He wanted to return to El Salvador, nonetheless, and was packing to go with the group. There was a mother of five who couldn't speak; she too was going back. Many were children, and some were old.

Music and art were well developed. There was always music—free songs on the guitar and singing. Most of the public buildings had murals painted on the outside walls.

J.F.R.

Colomoncagua, Honduras, December 1989

"NOW EACH OF US KNOWS ABOUT MALNUTRITION AND WE TEACH THE MOTHERS ABOUT GOOD NUTRITION" (Interview with Flora)

We never knew anything about nutrition. But when we came, there were a lot of people sick, especially children. A woman, Estella, came to meet with us, and others, too, to teach us about nutrition. We began at the bottom, and little by little we got a pot or a dish and kept working to be able to feed these children. Finally we made a house in one of the camps, and all the children went there to drink a glass of milk with oil in it. This was for kwashiorkor [severe malnutrition due to lack of protein].

Children with dry malnutrition are the ones who are very skinny; children with Kwashiorkor are those that are swollen up. We added oil to their milk so that the excess water in their bodies could come out. For dry malnutrition, we give the children everything we can—for example, all kinds of fruit, anything they bring here. But in the beginning, we had very little; maybe they brought a pineapple and we made a drink out of it, or we made *atole*. . . .

After Estella lots of nutritionists have come, and they

have taught us. Now each of us knows about malnutrition, and we teach the mothers about good nutrition. We work in a coordinated way with health and hygiene and the nutrition centers. . . .

I work as a mother for all of the orphans here, so that they will be bathed and well-fed. We have the orphans scattered throughout the camp and, along with other women, we help to care for the children. Here we are all mothers. So if a child is an orphan or if their own mother is sick, there is another woman to be the mother. That is how we work.

STEVE CAGAN: *Salvadoran refugees, Mesa Grande refugee camp, Honduras, August 1982.*

PART II

GOING HOME

DODY RIGGS

Chapter 3

"A ROSARY OF MEN, WOMEN, AND CHILDREN" RETURNING FROM MESA GRANDE

On four separate occasions, beginning in 1987, groups of refugees have left the camp at Mesa Grande in Honduras to make their way back to the villages in El Salvador. Sometimes they have walked; sometimes they have ridden. They have been accompanied by music of their own making, by international delegations, and by Salvadoran church people. They have spent countless hours in bureaucratic hassles at the border; on the road, they have been stopped and searched by army units.

The next pages tell the stories of these returns. The most difficult and longest was the last (October 1989). Negotiations for the buses and trucks that were to carry the refugees and their possessions stretched on for weeks. The rains came. Old folks died of exposure. Refugees started out on foot and were detained in an open pavilion at San Marcos for nine days. Salvadorans and internationals together went on a hunger strike to protest the delays. Once the vehicles arrived, it took four days to go 60 miles.

Yet, in spite of all, these are triumphant stories—the culmination and the commencement of a whole host of dreams.

Mesa Grande, Honduras, 1988

Santa Marta, El Salvador, October 1987

THE FIRST REPATRIATION: "THE REFUGEES WERE COMING AND THEY HAD BETTER GET READY!"

"A ROSARY OF MEN, WOMEN, AND CHILDREN"

With the signing of the Esquipulas II peace accords, refugees were given the right to repatriate to their places of origin. . . . When they informed officials of their wishes, they were told that returning as entire villages would be impossible, that it was dangerous, that nobody had done that before. During the ensuing nine months, the refugees held their ground, insisting that they were going to leave Mesa Grande on October 11, 1987, and return to El Salvador. Despite efforts by the Honduran government, the Salvadoran government, and the United Nations High Commission on Refugees, they were not to be dissuaded. One day shortly before their scheduled departure, a UNHCR official made a final effort to halt or delay their plans. But they stood firm, asserting that they were already packing and would not change their day of departure. Finally the UNHCR representative threw up her hands, climbed into her car, and drove to San Salvador to tell the government that the refugees were coming and they had better get ready!

K.H.

At 5:00 a.m. on October 10th, 4,313 Salvadoran refugees left Mesa Grande for their homeland. In El Salvador they were met by a caravan of buses and trucks organized by the Lutheran Church, the National Commission on Repopulation (CNR), the Archdiocese of San Salvador, Diaconia, Catholic Relief Services, and other religious and humanitarian organizations. [Ed.]

We did not know until the evening of October 9th whether or not internationals in El Salvador would be allowed to meet the refugees at the Honduran border. But at 10:00 that night, those who were going to the border met in the Lutheran church to finalize details. We divided ourselves up into five groups, one for each of the places to which the refugees were returning. At 3:30 in the morning, we formed a caravan of vehicles headed out for the border. On the other side of the border, the refugees, who also had not slept, were loading the trucks with their meager belongings—clothing and cooking pots rolled up into straw sleeping mats.

Our trip continued until 9:00 in the morning. The border was congested with people: international reporters, Salvadoran television crews, religious representatives, and others. We were all asked to remain at a distance until two

ADAM KUFELD: *Mesa Grande refugees arriving in El Salvador.*

military commanders arrived. Both appeared to be Americans.

Finally the refugees arrived at the border and the convoys got started. Many of the people were going to Santa Marta. When near their destination, they were told that the buses and trucks would go no further. Therefore, they had to carry their provisions into the village themselves. [Ed.]

After a moment the people began walking. It appeared impossible. I'm sure that in Europe or North America that would have been the attitude—it can't be done. We had to carry 50-pound sacks during a 45-minute walk over a rocky path, climbing up and down a mountain side. Some of the parcels were divided into smaller ones so the women and children could carry them. The spectacle was incredible, a rosary of men, women, children, old people carrying burdens on their heads and backs, which weighed many times as much as they. Some people fell, not being able to support the weight of their charges, or slipped on the treacherous slopes of the mountainside. With barely enough strength to carry ourselves, let alone the bundles, we continued on. Every time I met someone along the way they smiled. They showed so much strength, so much courage, and so much gentleness.

P.C.

ADAM KUFELD: *Leaving the Mesa Grande camp by bus, a woman carries her child into the outside world for the first time.*

Mesa Grande, Honduras, August 1988

"QUE VIVA EL SEGUNDO RETORNO! QUE VIVA EL PUEBLO REFUGIADO!"

The caravan that left the camp on Saturday morning, August 13th, consisted of 36 buses and well over 100 trucks provided by the United Nations. The lead bus, in which some of us rode, was for the musicians. Four guitarists and one bass player played music of El Salvador and accompanied the singing of songs, which had been composed by the community, including the children, for the return. The music alternated with chants, cheering the second return of the "refugee people": *"Que viva el segundo retorno! Que viva el pueblo refugiado!"* ("Long live the second return! Long live the refugee people!") And for us—*"Que viva la solidaridad international!"* ("Long live the international solidarity!") All of this was heard back down the line of buses because of a speaker, which it was my job to hold outside a window of the bus.

The other constant sound was the cheeping of chicks in crates at the back of the bus. These people move with their chickens. Amid all the austerity of camp life, which we shared for two nights, I shall remember the best bowl of chicken soup I ever tasted. It was prepared for us by a refugee family, and we ate it in the hut, with chickens constantly crossing the mud floor. Outside each row of huts were little covered roosts for the chickens, on poles about six feet high.

They entered by climbing a kind of ladder. I was fascinated by this, and I asked one of the young girls how many chickens lived in each of these roosts. *"Bastante,"* was her answer. "Enough."

It was the pride of this refugee community that was so astounding. In the caravan there were two symbols of their pride: the lead bus with the music and the tractor. When, after extended negotiations and a night spent sleeping on the side of the road, the convoy finally crossed the border, it was the blue and white Ford tractor that got the loudest cheers. It drove through the ranks of Salvadoran soldiers, armed with automatic rifles, and beneath the two US Army helicopters which had been circling the convoy. "Our tractor against your guns! Our will to farm again in our own land against your military strategies!"

In Central America a tractor is called a *chapulin*, a grasshopper, because like the little grasshopper it can chew up so much. The sight of that little tractor driving across the border immediately inspired members of the Going Home Campaign to raise money for a second *chapulin* for the returnees.

The refugee people moved with great pride and negotiated each step of the way with their own demands concerning the return. The UN was to give to each family the exact sum promised to them (money to tide them over for the first few weeks at home). The immigration authorities were not to require more forms to be filled out than what had already been provided to the UN. Above all, there was to be no interrogation of members of the community at the border. A slogan on the side of a bus read: *"Los criminales deben ser in-*

terrogados. No nosotros." ("Criminals should be interrogated. Not us.")

The refugees insisted on moving as a single unit and on returning to those areas which they themselves had chosen. They also insisted that *we* be allowed to accompany them all the way home and that the members of their families and the church people, with supplies of food for them in El Salvador, be allowed to join their convoy when they entered the land.

The Salvadoran government said no to these last two demands. Hundreds of people in El Salvador were stopped at a bridge outside of San Salvador by a frightening show of military force and prevented from coming to meet the returnees. We were not allowed to cross the border with them.

The refugee leadership had been pressing the demand for our accompaniment, as a measure to insure their safety from military harassment or governmental duplicity. But the government appeared to regard us as a great threat. In the Salvadoran press, the military fulminated against *los internacionalistas* and the danger we presented to internal order in El Salvador. We were, in fact, a humble crew, the 15 of us: a couple of Roman Catholic priests, a nun, a young Lutheran church worker, a Baptist pastor, a rabbi—not much of a threat to anyone, we were sure. Yet our presence seemed to work as a bargaining chip, other concessions being made so long as we did not cross the border.

It may well have been our presence, and what was being made of it in the media there, that enabled the refugee leadership to meet face to face at the border with the highest ranking officials of the government of El Salvador. One of the

BOB PERILLO: *"Our tractor against your guns!"*

ADAM KUFELD: *A young refugee woman is fingerprinted by a Salvadoran government official at the border.*

BOB PERILLO: *Buses prepared to leave Mesa Grande.*

refugee leaders compared it to David meeting Goliath. At that final negotiating session, the US Embassy and the UN were present as well as leaders of the churches of El Salvador. It was those church leaders who assumed the role that we were to have played, after the caravan crossed the border. They promised to accompany, to observe, and to advocate for the safe passage of the refugees.

The young men who composed the *directiva* of the refugee community reminded me of the leaders of groups like the Welfare Rights Organization in years past in the US. They consulted with their people and then they called the shots. They knew, as WRO leaders had known, that poor people can only succeed if they are bold and united in their demands—and that they must make demands! Otherwise what they are entitled to will be denied to them. International law guarantees their right to return home, so they act on that right. Assistance from the UN is their right as refugees, so they insist upon it in the exact amount agreed upon. Now in El Salvador they will assert their right as citizens to participate in the political life of their country, no matter how the ruling forces there may feel about that.

D.G.

*Mesa Grande, Honduras/Tremedal,
El Salvador, October 1989*

"WE ARE RETURNING HOME. . . AFTER NINE YEARS OF CAPTIVITY"

I flew to Houston to meet up with 12 other delegates who had also dropped everything to go on this emergency mission to accompany refugees from Mesa Grande to their homelands in El Salvador. We had been monitoring the repatriation from our eight cities: calling the Washington Going Home office for updates, calling rapid response networks, and calling Congressional offices, as we heard of the Salvadoran government's and the UN's obstruction of this fourth return.

The Salvadoran government had refused to allow the refugees to cross the border without proper documentation. The military had insisted that each refugee of the 1,400 returning (most of them children) fill out a four-and-a-half page document, including all family names and addresses, all contacts with the FMLN, their *noms de guerre* while fighting with the FMLN, and their reasons for wanting to return home. The refugees had agreed to fill out a one-page form.

The refugees had made plans to leave Mesa Grande on the 14th of October, had packed up their belongings, disassembled their wooden houses and loaded them, and cooked food for a five or six days' journey. When the agreement fell

HARVEY FINKLE: *Refugees from Mesa Grande walk to San Marcos.*

apart, they made the first of many courageous independent decisions, trusting that if they acted, others would be forced to react and be held accountable by the international community. Several hundred of them would start to walk to El Salvador, stopping at the town of San Marcos, four hours away.

The march to San Marcos, accompanied by half of the 15 North Americans already in Honduras, was slow and rainy. There were many children and old people, and the road was rocky and rutted. Honduran military escorted them.

After a brief meeting with the UN staff, the refugees were offered a church hall for the night. They passed into the one-room large hall, and the Honduran military and the UN staff locked the doors behind them. They were not allowed out for the next nine days. There was one toilet for the 300 of them who stayed (some having decided to return to the camp), no food, no water, no blankets. It was 45 degrees at night and windy. Some North Americans were originally allowed to go back and forth to get supplies from local vendors, then later, no longer allowed in or out.

At the camp there were still approximately 800 refugees without houses or a means to cook, waiting for permission to leave. Many were sick with the flu; two old people had died from exposure and one child from a drowning accident. Finally food and blankets were supplied to the camp and to San Marcos. Three additional latrines were added to the church hall. Still, diarrhea and dehydration were rampant.

Eventually documentation was agreed upon (one page), and the buses were again available. But there were still com-plications. The UN had broken its word to supply a tractor to the repopulated town of Santa Marta, and the refugees now stated that they would not allow the buses to roll until they got the tractor. That took another day or two, but they got it. At this point, they heard of our coming and insisted that the caravan wait until we arrived.

We did arrive, were hugged, and the buses started to roll. They left so quickly, seven of us were left chatting in the dark in the road and had to flag down the last bus to jump aboard. It was cold and damp. People were in shirts and cotton dresses. Their faces were dazed and exhausted and numb. I gave one shivering and frightened looking six-year-old girl my suit jacket. She seemed most interested in the fact that my mother had made it.

One minor victory in our trip had been getting a shipment of infant formula through Honduran customs. We had received word that the refugees needed formula badly, as many of the mothers' milk supply had dried up with the lack of water and food. We held onto the baggage claim for the 16 cartons of milk we bought just before departure and prayed they would be given back to us. Customs told us they could only give them to us if we could produce the receipt from the supermarket. (Of course, we didn't have it.) Our guide thought to say that the formula had been especially requested by a particular Bishop, but they didn't believe that. I asked if they had a phone that we could use to call the Bishop. They paused. I insisted. We got the milk.

On the first night of the caravan, we slept in El Poy, about ten minutes from the border. The tension and fatigue

HARVEY FINKLE: *Communication of plans during repatriation.*

balanced each other out; all of us, if we thought about it, expected the *directiva* to protect us from the ever-present military. At 5:30 we were up and rolling towards the border, where it turned out that we would wait for arrangements to be made until 4:30 that afternoon. People were patient and unquestioning, trusting in the elected *directiva* and in the coordinators (one for each of 35 buses). We bought delicious large oranges and bananas and sweet breads from the local Honduran vendors which we gave to the bus coordinators to distribute to the children.

Four of our delegation were not allowed to pass into El Salvador. (They did not have Salvadoran visas.) They found lodging locally and waited for word from us. Three others had visas about to expire, as they had been in Mesa Grande for two weeks; later they were told they couldn't cross into El Salvador. At 2:00 p.m. we were seated in our assigned buses, ready to go, when the leader of the first delegation, from Madison, Wisconsin, and five other delegates had their bus drawn out of fifth place in line and brought into the border area. The Treasury Police, reputedly one of the worst security forces in El Salvador, insisted the five North Americans get off the bus. They refused. A reporter (actually, a military man disguised as a reporter) interviewed them, then asked for a picture of them in the doorway of the bus. They assembled in the doorway, and the military grabbed them.

I spoke to Pedro, one of the *directiva* from Guarjila or Corral de Piedra. He was calm about the six delegates being held by the Treasury Police; he said they weren't going anywhere.

In fact, this gave the refugees a chance for face-to-face negotiations which they'd been waiting for all day. Why? They wanted Julio Menendez (a leader from one of the repopulated villages) and six church workers, picked up on their return to San Salvador from coming to visit the refugees, released immediately. They also wanted the 800 people from San Salvador, who had come up to meet them on buses and who were being detained at Colima, to be allowed to meet with them on their return.

Pedro felt that it was better to negotiate at the border than in El Salvador. It was costing the UN $6,700 a day to delay the repopulation; the refugees had the buses and the visibility now. He was unsmiling, calm, decisive, and intelligent. Two experienced Salvadorans in our group were laughing and joking, trying to get us food, telling us to keep calm and leave all the political decisions to the *directiva*. Our job was merely to accompany, not to lead.

By 4:30 p.m., the six North Americans were released, but we (the internationals) were told we could have only 72 hours in the country—an order expressly from President Cristiani.

It was an enormous relief to see all 35 buses assembled in a large circle over the border. We arranged shifts of four people to patrol during the night. We assumed the *directiva* was patrolling as well. I got the 8:00 to 10:00 shift, and then climbed into the aisle of a Guarjila bus and dropped immediately off to sleep. The bus noises were comforting and intimate: old people sighing and whispering to spouses; children coughing and talking to their mothers; chickens in

BOB PERILLO: *Refugees gather to negotiate.*

their cages on top of the buses scratching on the roof; and occasionally people whispering, "Don't step on the internationals." (Out of courtesy all North Americans are called internationals, which is, of course, a compliment.)

The following day we were assigned to individual buses, with nine of us going to Teocinte, five to Guarjila, and five to Santa Marta. We were told that these were, in fact, not the actual destinations, as the refugees were hoping to avoid a waiting army presence. They would eventually move to small villages near these already populated towns.

I went to Teocinte. We drove in a caravan to the heavily militarized town of Tejutla, where the buses lined three streets of an intersection. It was the first time the buses were headed in three different directions, and it reminded us that people would soon be saying goodbye to family and friends they had lived, suffered, and triumphed with for nine years.

As we waited again for negotiations over the release of the seven, and reunion with the waiting 800, local church groups brought us rice, beans, and tortillas. They had been cooking for our group of 1,400 for the past five days, every day cooking the same amount. A Jesuit North American priest, who had recently lost his Salvadoran permanent resident status for political work, but who refused to leave the country, was there. Other priests, Catholic and Protestant, were also there. We had a joyful day, swimming and shampooing in the river, laughing and rejoicing at the sight of so many Salvadoran children under age nine, born in a refugee camp, who had never swum in a river, and never been in their homeland. They splashed, shouted, and did flips off the rocks. The women bathed in their underpants and slips. The North American women bathed fully dressed, but everyone went in.

We learned at 6:00 that night that the six church workers had been released. There was an agonizing debate among the *directiva* over whether to refuse to move until Menendez was released as well and risk both greater hardship to the many sick children and elderly and having the Salvadoran military intervene, or to move on and continue to hope international pressure would succeed at freeing their leader and friend. (This would be the fourth time he was captured. He is 35, well-known in the US where he has toured, and a national leader of the repopulation movement.)

The *directiva* met well into the night and decided at last to move on. They asked some of us to go to visit Menendez' lawyer and the judge who would hear his case when we arrived in San Salvador.

The ecumenical service that night in the middle of the intersection was dedicated to Julio Menendez and was the last service when we were all together. The UN trucks repeatedly drove through, stopping close to the speakers with their motors running, making it hard to hear. The military, however, had backed off somewhat after Pedro told them, "North Americans don't like all those guns pointed in their faces."

Saturday morning the three Teocinte buses left the intersection first. We didn't know it, but the other buses refused to move until they had word we had safely reached our destination. (There was the most concern for Teocinte, as it was the smallest group—88 people—and the location was the most isolated.)

On the other side of Tejutla, we pulled into a military encirclement on a large field. There were many UN staff people, including one UN woman with a video camera taking pictures of the refugees' faces and our faces. It was very hot and dusty, and the refugees had to move all of their belongings from the buses to open pick-up trucks as the roads were too poor for the buses to proceed. The soldiers had angry-looking dogs on leashes sniffing all the refugees' luggage. They allowed the dogs to urinate on the luggage, and we noticed that the dogs answered only to English commands.

The military captains were seen pointing at individual refugees and writing notes next to their names. The *comandante* gave a chilling welcome speech, addressing them as fellow-countrymen whom they were happy to welcome, and then announced there would be a roll call. Only after the refugees heard their names could they enter the buses.

Since six men from Teocinte had walked down to greet us in Tejutla, circumventing the military barriers, we worried about what would happen to them if they could not return with us. We were able to smuggle them into the buses, however, because there was little attention paid as to who got into what bus and when.

We spent the next hour bouncing back and forth in hot, dusty, noisy open trucks. The mountains were breathtakingly beautiful; the small clusters of houses had flowering vines and blossoming poinsettia trees. We stopped in the town of St. Ignacio outside a school, and one of the *directiva*, Mauricio, shouted from a megaphone, "We are Salvadorans! We are returning home to Teocinte after nine years of captivity in a refugee camp. We are *campesinos* like you. We are Salvadorans like you. *Viva* the children of St. Ignacio! *Viva* the children of Teocinte! *Viva* the fourth return!"

The arrival into Tremedal, our final destination, was joyful and took us by surprise. We realized after yet one more stop that we needed to get out and walk up the road to be finally home. There were tearful, joyous reunions; Mauricio was reunited with a five-year-old son that had left with his mother on a prior repopulation, 14 months earlier. He introduced me proudly to his elderly father who had been waiting for him. Sisters, cousins, sons, and fathers were reunited, and the Teocinte townspeople had brought water and lunch. Their material and moral support would prove invaluable over the next few weeks.

We took over a large, empty church floor. Families staked out different areas, hanging hammocks, getting water jugs distributed. People were exhausted, and many were quite sick. The chickens in their crates (about 30 crates) were put in a shady area atop a small hill. The 12 or 15 pigs were put in an abandoned stone building that had walls but had lost its roof to a bomb. There were adobe houses, half-bombed, half-standing, and there were seven adobe houses with tile roofs that housed the seven families of Tremedal. These families were hopeful about the resources the new people would bring—schools, health promoters, housing, and food supplies. They were worried, however, about the military harassment they would invite by their presence.

ADAM KUFELD: *Trucks are loaded during the night for an early morning departure.*

BOB PERILLO: *"Long live the hunger strike caused by the delay of the 4th Return!"*

BOB PERILLO: *The trip home.*

BOB PERILLO: *Unloading in El Salvador.*

We ended the first day in Tremedal with a triumphant mass. James, a young Scottish priest who lived in the area, led the communion service. He talked eloquently of the people's faith and their courage in their homecoming. He spoke of the importance of the repopulation to the country and of the strong message sent by their peaceful reclaiming of their homes. We stood exhausted in a large, mostly dark, adobe church, with the bright light from the lantern shining on those closest to the altar.

G.W.

LAURA JACKSON: *The first truck out of Colomoncagua, December 1989.*

Chapter 4

"WE COULD SEE EL SALVADOR ACROSS THE VALLEY"
RETURNING FROM COLOMONCAGUA

The entire Colomoncagua camp of 8,400 refugees repatriated to the province of Morazan in El Salvador between November of 1989 and March of 1990. After countless delays in their plans, the first group *walked* home on November 18th without official permission from the Salvadoran government or official assistance from the UNHCR. Once in Morazan they got busy making preparations for the groups that would follow.

The refugees back in Colomoncagua were still facing delays. But they found an ally in a strange place—the Honduran army headquarters. The Honduran government was eager to be rid of the burden of these Salvadorans in exile, so with a little persuasion they became complicitors in the repatriation effort, supplying trucks (the leasing of which was paid for by humanitarian organizations) and a military escort for the second *retorno*. Inspired by the success of these first efforts, other groups of refugees quickly followed suit and the camp closed down by late February.

In this chapter you will find a detailed account of the second *retorno*, an interview with the *directiva* from Colomoncagua just before this second return, and the personal reflections of a North American woman who was visiting the camp in December and walked with refugees to the Salvadoran border.

LAURA JACKSON: *Girls at Colomoncagua.*

Colomoncagua, Honduras, December 1989

"LOOK AT THOSE WHO HAVE ALREADY GONE BACK . . . THEY ARE WORKING" (Interview with the *Directiva* Before the Second Return)

It's been more than six months since we planned the repatriation. We didn't know that things were going to get so bad in Salvador [referring to the offensive]. And we had agreed with the government on our return date. So, given the situation we are in, how many more months can we put up with these conditions. The malnutrition is growing—now it's at 34 percent. The people don't feel like they are here any more; they sense that they are on the road home. And how can we maintain this community? . . .

We don't know why they would renege now. We know that the situation there is difficult, but our situation here is going to get much worse. Wait and see how things are three months down the line with no work, everyone standing around looking at one another. But if we are home. . . . Look at those who have already gone back on the 18th of November; they are working and that gives us all the more desire to go back. Here we are just waiting with our arms crossed. The summer months are short and if we don't go back now, we'll arrive in the winter with no homes. If we don't build the houses now and prepare the fields for planting, then we will need to live on outside assistance for another year or more . . . .

Here we are a community that lives on outside assistance. But when we go back to Salvador, we won't have that assistance and we will be a developing community. Many things will be quite different for us. Some structures may have to be more autonomous; we may have to find ways to promote production in all the different areas of work. But the important thing is that each person be responsible to see that things work for the good of the whole community.

We know that it will be a little different because here there is no commerce; here everyone works, but no one gains a salary; there is no circulation of money. But there, commerce functions; our goods will have to go on the market. So we will have to be very careful there; we don't know what effect money will have. We'll have to be even more careful about administering the goods of the community. Those who work, supposedly, should gain a salary. But one of the benefits of working in community is to give continuity to the projects that we have started. . . .

One of the problems we see is that the majority of the children have never seen money, and they may waste it, buying things they don't really need. They will be learning. Those who came when they were eight or nine years old now are eighteen, and they really don't know how to deal with having money.

Another problem is that the youth don't know how to do agricultural work. They only know how to work as artisans. So if we can't get the workshops going, that will be a big problem.

Colomoncagua, Honduras, December 1989

"THERE THEY WERE, THOSE 30 WONDERFUL TRUCKS ROARING INTO THE CAMPS"

"The trucks are coming! The trucks are coming!" Hundreds of children ran up the hill on the dusty road, while down in the little valley the whole community came out of their huts to look. Everybody was grinning, smiling, laughing. Everybody was pointing to the long line of trucks, moving slowly down the unpaved road in the uncertain light of dusk with their lights already on. After nine years of waiting, on Saturday the 9th of December 1989, the trucks had indeed arrived at the Salvadoran refugee camp in Colomoncagua, Honduras, and their arrival was like another proof of the determination of the refugees to control their own destiny. Tired of waiting and of broken promises, the refugees had now decided they could wait no more: they were going

LAURA JACKSON: *Trucks are cheered as they leave the camp.*

to go back to their homeland, to El Salvador, and they would take along all the individual and community goods they had accumulated throughout their exile. That was what the trucks were for.

How did this come about? On May 29th, during an international meeting on refugee problems held in Guatemala, the UNHCR agreed that the repatriation of Colomoncagua would begin on November 27th and be over before Christmas 1989. The place of resettlement would be Meanguera in the north of Morazan. A group of about 200 refugees would repatriate early on November 9th to prepare conditions for the rest of the community.

As part of the agreement with the new right-wing ARENA government, a group of 17 functionaries from the Salvadoran department of immigration moved to the camps and began issuing temporary documentation to the refugees. By the middle of November, the refugees had dismantled all of the infrastructure of the camps. Workshops, clinics, school, churches were all packed and ready to go. Only the houses were left standing.

The 9th of November came around, but the UNHCR was not ready to send the first 200 people. Nor was it ready on the 10th or the 11th. On the 11th, the guerrillas launched their great offensive and the UNHCR declared that, given the conditions in El Salvador, it was forced to delay the repatriation. The refugees felt deceived once again. "War is nothing new in our country," they said. "If we wait for peace, we'll never go. We want to go there now and help in the process of peace."

Unwilling to wait any longer, a group of 1,100 refugees left, walking for El Salvador only a few kilometers away. It was an act of incredible daring. The Honduran army and the UNHCR, taken completely by surprise by that long line of men, women, and children singing and carrying on their shoulders as much as they could of their possessions, tried fruitlessly to stop them, and ended up escorting them to the border [from which the refugees proceeded to their homelands in Morazan].

The response of the Salvadoran government was swift: the vice-president of the republic himself, who only a few weeks earlier had visited the camps and had promised the refugees a safe return, now declared all repatriation suspended, and accused the refugees of going back to fight with the FMLN. The team of Salvadoran immigration officials was immediately withdrawn, having issued documents to only about half of the remaining 8,400 refugees.

Mr. Fouinat, representative of the UNHCR in Honduras, immediately announced that, as long as the Salvadoran government was opposed to it, no return could take place. It seemed that the repatriation process was really stalled for good this time. But the refugees were not of the same opinion. With all of the infrastructure dismantled, life in the camps had become absolutely impossible.

A mass of people, who had been accustomed to work and produce, to be active, to struggle every day for their survival, were not going to remain idle for God knows how long. How to overcome this last apparently insurmountable hurdle?

There was reason to believe that the Honduran army

LAURA JACKSON: *A child sits by his family's possessions.*

RENATO CARMADA: *"Mr. Fouinat (of the UNHCR) announced that as long as the Salvadoran government was opposed to it, no return could take place. . . . But the refugees were not of the same opinion." R.C.*

would allow another repatriation like the one that had taken place on November 18th. It was common knowledge that the Honduran government wanted the Salvadoran refugees to leave Honduras as soon as possible. They had never wanted them in their territory. But would they be willing to antagonize the Salvadoran government and let them go?

Why not ask Retired Colonel Abraham Turcios, head of the Honduran National Commission for Refugees, directly for permission to repatriate but with trucks this time around so they could take along their individual and community possessions? A delegation formed by two of the many foreign visitors who had come to the camps to assist in the repatriation was asked to go and talk to the colonel, cautiously inquiring about his disposition. It was no small thing the refugees were asking: if the Honduran government agreed, it would do so against the wishes of the UNHCR and those of the Salvadoran government. The only thing the refugees could count upon was the coincidence of their desire to go with the desire of the Honduran government to see them go.

After three meetings, the colonel asked: "And how many trucks do the refugees want?" The permission had been granted by the highest level of the government and the army!

And now there they were, those 30 wonderful trucks, beautifully rolling down the hill, roaring into the camps, enthusiastically welcomed by a population which, through years of pain and struggle, had learned how to defend themselves with cunning and strength, and were not willing to be dominated any longer by anybody. The trucks, paid for by a number of humanitarian organizations, had arrived. The

RENATO CARMADA: *Honduran military escort refugees out of Colomoncagua.*

night was spent in feverish preparations: this time only 500 people would leave. Beds, tables, machinery were loaded.

At 6:00 the following morning, the caravan left, personally led by Colonel Turcios himself. After the trucks, the people left, walking. Later two trucks would come back and get the elderly, the pregnant women, and the children who could not afford the eight-kilometer walk. Escorted by an army patrol, the people marched through the Honduran town of Colomoncagua, thanking the local population as they passed, greeted by the passersby, by the people who had run out of their houses to see them pass. Many old people told them: "God bless you." A musical group appeared out of nowhere and played for the returning refugees.

By 5:00 p.m., the whole operation was finished. At the other side of the border, the first group, who had repatriated on November 18th, were waiting for their fellow ex-refugees. They had been the ones who had fixed the road on the Salvadoran side. They had rented, with the help of international organizations, the eight trucks that were now waiting on the Salvadoran border. They were helping to unload and load the trucks. These were not terrorists, as the Salvadoran government had claimed; they were people who wanted most of all to rebuild the community.

"This has been a model repatriation!" Colonel Turcios exclaimed at the end of the day. Not one incident had occurred.

R.C.

Colomoncagua, Honduras, December 1989

"WE COULD SEE EL SALVADOR ACROSS THE VALLEY, ALWAYS IN SIGHT"

Around 9:00 a.m. the 30 trucks labored up the hill and out of the camp. The oldest men were settled in the back; the oldest women and the youngest babies (one born the day before) were packed into the cabs with the Honduran drivers. Everyone else making the repatriation that day would walk the eight miles carrying with them the smaller household items and supplies they would need for the day. Many of the women carried young children; young boys carried their family's chickens tucked under an arm or—if there were a few—in small wooden cages balanced on their shoulders.

For awhile I carried a six-year-old girl. Although we had left the camp in a large group, by this time we had formed two single lines moving along the shoulders of the road. I was aware mostly of the sounds of the leather workshoes on the dirt and of the quiet. We could see El Salvador across the valley, always in sight. I thought about the child I was carrying—that this was the first time in her life she had been outside of the camps. I wondered what she was thinking, where would home be for her, and why she had so easily let me raise her onto my hip.

LAURA JACKSON: *Leaving Colomoncagua, December 1989.*

LAURA JACKSON: *The road from Colomoncagua to the Salvadoran border.*

We were being escorted by the Honduran military. At one point, we passed through a military checkpoint and under the single wooden pole that had been raised for us. When one of the soldiers would come especially near, the child I carried would tighten her arms around my neck and pull her head even closer to mine. "Soldiers," she would whisper, her lips touching my ear, and as easily as I could I would respond, "Yes, soldiers," and I'd boost her higher on my hip and walk on. Attached to her dress with a safety pin was a small piece of paper on which were printed her name and the number of her household.

We stopped for a rest. The woman next to me peeled two potatoes and gave one to each of her children. There was a small pool of water alongside the road and boys were taking their chickens over and pushing their beaks into it. A child started to cry because one of his chickens had died in its cage. I do not think he was crying for grief as much as for shame that he had failed in his responsibility. After some discussion, the dead chicken was left by the side of the road and we gathered up the children, the plastic containers of fuel, the washbuckets, and the food and continued in silence toward the border.

L.J.

JOHN GRANT: *Refugee child, El Salvador.*

PART III

LIFE IN THE VILLAGES

JOHN GRANT: *An international visitor notes, with regard to the children, "When we arrived, we brought 1,100 oranges. As soon as the truck stopped, children swarmed all over it. I thought the oranges were gone, but I found out the children put them in the storeroom. Two hours later, one orange each was given to every member (1,100) of the community."*

Chapter 5

"THE FRUIT OF THEIR OWN TREES"
A DESCRIPTION OF VILLAGE LIFE

This chapter allows you to visit the repopulated communities, along with North Americans who have made that pilgrimage. Here you will see faith in action. You will read about recovering the past and building the future. You will find out about pig projects and agricultural production. You will read about folk singers and rural teachers. You will meet one woman who knew exactly where to find the corn grinding stone she buried when she fled nearly a decade before.

In these pages you will discover how the organizing that the refugees did while in the camps is paying off. You will see how the skills that they developed through various workshops are being used in village projects. You will also become aware of the problems they face and of their needs for health care, clean water, and schools.

There is a lot to admire in the way these ex-refugees have begun to live their lives with dignity in the repopulated villages. There is a lot to fear in their continual confrontations with an army that would prefer they live elsewhere or not be alive at all. There is a lot to learn about how they assure the basic needs of all of their people and what their accomplishments as a people can mean for other communities, including our own.

SCOTT WRIGHT: *Children await their turn at the Martin Luther King Health Clinic, funded in part by churches of Madison, Wisconsin.*

"THERE ARE FIVE HEALTH PROMOTERS, MOST OF WHOM ARE YOUNG PEOPLE"

We have a clinic here where we can treat most normal injuries and illnesses. There are five health promoters, most of whom are young people, and one woman who is responsible, and who has no children of our own. When I first arrived, I helped the health promoters to weigh the children under five years of age. We discovered three children under two years of age with severe malnutrition. Since then, we've been working with the mothers to improve the diets of these children.

On the 22nd of December, we had another baby die—the second since the refugees arrived here. This one had been born the day before the people left Mesa Grande. We were unable to get an autopsy, so we really don't know why he died. The baby's sister of one-and-a-half years arrived in Copapayo with kwashiorkor—a severe case of malnutrition from lack of protein. She is starting to recover but her baby brother, who appeared to be in perfect health, died.

I now have concern when the food shipments are held up by the military that the children who are borderline malnourished are beginning to lose weight. I was reminded that when the people repopulated San Jose las Flores, several children died the first couple of months because the food donations were not permitted to pass.

M.G.

Guarjila, El Salvador, March 1988

"I THINK PEOPLE CAME HOME FOR THE PAPAYAS, FOR THE FRUIT OF THEIR OWN TREES"

Our six days in Guarjila and the neighboring community of San Antonio los Ranchos were magic. A hammock—my first—very comfortable. Waking up at dawn to see a rooster and his minions parading on the roof of the next house. The grinding of corn on wonderful stone slabs for the obligatory, fat, and delicious Salvadoran tortillas at each meal. We heard of a woman, who upon returning, paced off from the well, dug, and uncovered her stone which she had buried when she fled.

The papayas—I think people came home for the papayas, for the fruit of their own trees, ripe and lush. Gardens, fruitful in just six months, watered by hand from

JOHN GRANT: *Early conditions in a repatriated village.*

LAURA JACKSON: *A recently rebuilt home with porch and clay oven for baking.*

buckets carried a quarter mile from the single tap. Fields cleared, stroke by stroke by machete, for beans and corn, readied for planting when the rains came in May. The daily grinding and sharpening of the machetes in front of each house while the morning frijoles and coffee heat on the fire. Salvadoran pigs, weird and albino, able to withstand six dry months, in and out of houses. And building, building. There were no houses when the people came home. No latrines. No clinic

We walked one morning to the site of the old town. Ruins there of the bombed church; vines growing over the half-of-a-porch left of a stone house. Time to reflect on whatever in the world it could be that impelled soldiers to drop bombs, to utterly destroy a tiny hamlet, two hours' walk from the nearest store or newspaper or hospital. These *are* dangerous villagers, however, because they have hope. They are reclaiming their land.

P.W.

Guarjila, El Salvador, April 1989

"GOVERNMENT REPRESSION DROVE THEM TO UNITY, LIKE A FIST"

Our elation at reaching our goal is tempered by a curious welcome. The village is festooned with signs that read, "Guarjila welcomes the international solidarity delegation from Finlandia." Have we come this far only to be upstaged by a bunch of Finns? Crestfallen at first, we later discover the welcome truly is intended for us; only Philadelphia has been translated as Finlandia.

Alejandro narrates the extraordinary history of the village. They fled persecution—"Our only crime was being poor and asking for justice"—to become refugees in Honduras in 1979. But the refugee camps were little better, and they chose to return home in October 1987.

Since then they have organized village life into eight sectors—construction, education, etc.—and have built 325 houses for the more than 2,000 residents, plus planting over 1,000 communally-owned acres in corn, beans, and rice. They have an open-air school, a small health clinic, and a pastoral building, and they are extremely proud of their pure water (which we see running from several standpipes).

Lunch—never have tortillas, rice, eggs, and coffee tasted so good. The food is prepared by three women, one of whom

RON MORGAN: *International visitors being fed at a village guest house.*

JOHN GRANT: *A visitor's travel note: "I was particularly impressed with the children. . . . Rosa was 12 years old. She had witnessed so many things in her life, many of them fearful, yet here she was in school, viewing her village with hope."* S.G.

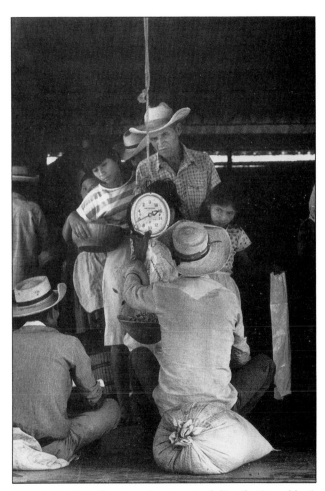

JOHN GRANT: *Community-organized distribution of food.*

grinds corn on a concave stone identical to the ones depicted in pre-Columbian figurines.

A leisurely tour of the village reveals an extraordinary degree of cooperative social organization. Apart from small gardens adjacent to family dwellings, land appears to be owned and worked communally. More surprising is the miniature garment factory crowded into a masonry building. Here collectivism has altered the usual sexual division of labor, because instead of male cutters (high status and pay) feeding female operatives (low status and pay), there is one cutter of each sex giving cloth to three men and three women bent over sewing machines. But gender has not totally disappeared—women make dresses; men make pants—which are distributed according to need. There is no cash exchange. It is pure cooperation.

Our guide explains they learned cooperation from two experiences. First and foremost, living in refugee camps compelled the villagers to cooperate, since many were orphans or disabled who had to rely on others for survival. Second, government repression drove them to unity, like a fist.

A.D.

Corral de Piedra (renamed Comunidad Ignacio Ellacuria), El Salvador, October 1989

"CLASSES MAY BEGIN OUTSIDE UNDER THE TREES"

Corral de Piedra is a small village of about 40 houses located halfway between the repopulated communities of Guarjila and San Jose las Flores, a good location. It lies on a main road. The main "street" through the town is a loop that connects with the main road. The street is lined on each side by a rock wall, hence the name, Corral de Piedra. The loop is roughly 300 meters long and 200 meters wide. Most of the houses are laid along this loop, especially on the northeast (far) side, where the small church and school were. It is by the church and school that the only three working *pilas* (sinks with faucet) are found.

Of the 40 houses it seems that only two were left undamaged by the widespread bombing of 1980 and 1981. They happen to be the two that were built of concrete blocks and finished with tile floors. One of these houses lies along the main road and has become the community food and animal feed *bodega* (warehouse). The pig pen is a few meters from the *bodega*. The other block house sits on the north corner of the loop. It is the general equipment and supplies *bodega*, and may also house the sewing cooperative to begin with. The house is in very good condition.

JOHN GRANT: *A returning Salvadoran surveys the wreckage of a church.*

JOHN GRANT: *Military grafitti on the wall of an abandoned building.*

Between 500 and 600 people now live in Corral de Piedra in about 100 families. Houses will be built one deep on each side of the loop and main road, beginning in spaces where there are no ruined houses, and leaving enough space between houses for gardens and animals, as is the custom. There are *tabla* (1 x 10s), *lamina* (tin sheets), and posts brought from Mesa Grande for building houses. These supplies are not expected to be enough, however, for all the houses needed. One house was nearly complete when I left the village the morning of November 2nd.

There are many immediate needs in Corral de Piedra. First of all is water. The three existing *pilas* barely provide water for drinking, cooking, and bathing. And many people have to walk nearly 500 meters for water. Water for washing and construction is presently not sufficient. There is one small stream that goes through the middle of the town, providing some water for bathing and washing. But it may dry up in a few months.

The health promoters that have been in the other repopulated communities for the past number of months will be taking turns helping the community of Corral de Piedra. Eventually the community hopes to build or create a health center. They are also talking about school possibilities. Classes may begin outside under the trees.

T.L.

SHARE: *A primary goal for each village is a community water system.*

JOHN GRANT: *Reconstruction by traditional methods in a repopulated village.*

ADAM KUFELD: *Woman building a house.*

JOHN GRANT: *A visitor notes: "I was completely amazed by the beauty and the design of everything . . . the school benches and desks, everthing hand hewn and nicely proportioned . . . the school area up on the hill, an umbrella of trees surrounding it and the blackboard propped up against the trees." V.B.*

RICK REINHARD: *The growing of their own food is the hallmark of self-sufficiency and empowerment for which each repopulated community aspires.*

Teocinte, El Salvador, October 1989

"NOW WE HAVE CALVES, ONE PAIR OF OXEN, AND WE ARE VERY GRATEFUL FOR THE TRUCK"

The town of Teocinte is picturesque, peaceful, and shady. Cobblestone streets wind up a steep hill; the village square has a large outspreading tree with a circular cement bench that wraps around the tree trunk. Posters celebrating their first anniversary as a town and declaring their human right to repatriate are everywhere. One sign reads: "Thanks be to God for our sister city that helps us—Arlington."

The three *directiva* members that we met with were Luis, about 45 and with a withered hand, Juan, 25, and Paz, 23 or 25. There are seven members of the *directiva*. The community of about 300 people is organized into two sectors. They wanted to give us a history of their year of resettlement, to tell us about ongoing projects:

In the beginning the construction looked difficult; we were few. We are almost through now. We repaired and built houses, schools, warehouses, and rebuilt the road. We have planted 40 *manzanas* of corn (somewhat over 80 acres). We replaced the church roof that had bullet holes. We feel positive about the water system and about the road. With aid from international solidarity we have 12 cows; now we have calves, one pair of oxen, and we are very grateful for the truck. This truck has helped us overcome a lot of difficulties; it has been an emergency ambulance and hauled food for the community.

We now have a preschool, a kindergarten, and an elementary school. Alice, a North American woman, helps in the school, and we have popular education—that is, the townspeople teach. Currently we have a child care project that needs financial backing. We have the toys but we need the provisions of food for the 55 to 60 children that might attend. We have a health project and an electrical generator project that we will present to CORDES for possible funding.

G.W.

RON MORGAN: *A young girl assists in the daily ritual of washing clothes.*

Jocoaitique, El Salvador, December 1989

"WE HAVE COME HERE. . . TO WORK FOR ALL OF OUR NECESSITIES" (Interview with Rosaria)

My name is Rosaria. I am one of the people who repatriated on the 18th of November from Colomoncagua. Now, in our own country, we feel very contented; now we can move from one place to another. For now, we are staying in the town of Jocoaitique, and since no institution has come to help us—with food, for example—it is PADECOMSM that is helping us. [PADECOMSM is a local organization for the development of the communities of Morazan.] They are the ones who are making sure that we all eat. And so far we are doing better than when we were in the camps.

Now we are getting six tortillas a day; in the camps it was only three. So we are doing well! And we hope that with the help of all of the communities of northern Morazan we will continue to do well. We are also coordinating with them [PADECOMSM] how to be most effective in our work. For instance, in the three weeks we have been here, we have been working together with the communities of northern Morazan in the places where we will be living. People come there to work with us from the different communities; up to 500 have come to work with us. So every day there is a large number of people who are working in the places where we will be resettled.

We have been organizing ourselves in the different work that needs to be done. We said that we wanted to bring with us the form of work and organization that we learned in Colomoncagua. So we are already working in education, in health, and in the workshops. For example, basket weaving—we've made 105 baskets already! And we didn't have anything at all to start with. We are fixing shoes and mending clothes. We are working in all the things we did there. We have heard some news broadcasts that are really lies; it isn't like they say—that we have come to join the FMLN. We aren't with one side or the other. And we want that to be clear on the international level. We have come here to set up our work and to work for all of our necessities.

Ciudad Segundo Montes, El Salvador, August 1990

"THEY REPRESENT A GREAT HOPE FOR EL SALVADOR"

When Father Segundo Montes visited the Colomoncagua refugee camp in Honduras, the children followed him as if he were a pied piper. Part of the attraction was the fact that he owned something they had never seen before—an umbrella.

He was to go on to shelter them from more than rain. His studies on refugee dynamics, published out of the Jesuit University in San Salvador, so publicized the accomplishments of the Colomoncagua population that when they returned to northern Morazan, one short month after Father Montes was brutally murdered by the Salvadoran army, they found that they were already well known in their native land.

On March 25, 1990, the five resettled communities named themselves Ciudad Segundo Montes, not just to honor a martyr, but to remind themselves that they have the responsibility to live up to his conviction that they represented a great hope for El Salvador.

The visitor to Ciudad Segundo Montes knows that they are succeeding. After eight short months, the water and sewage systems are in place; schools meet regularly; workshops producing children's sweaters, leather work, hammocks, bricks, and ceramic water jugs are in place (sewing, engine mechanics, shoe, and sombrero workshops are under construction), and the collective chicken farm is not only producing two eggs per inhabitant (about 8,400) per week, but also a modest cash flow from the sale of the excess.

Beyond physical and economic development, the emerging social and community structure of Ciudad Segundo Montes is equally impressive. A highly participatory governance system monitors a fair distribution of goods and handles problems of alcoholism, family violence, school curriculum, the rights of women, while responding as well to the continuing problems of forced recruitment and military harassment.

All of this came together for me in a long conversation with Maria Lopez, coordinator of the Committee of Mothers. Women are important in Ciudad Segundo Montes, not only statistically (they make up two-thirds of the adult population), but also in their transformational thinking. For they have come to see the importance of who they are—as life givers, as nurturers of life, as thinkers, as leaders, as lobbyists. They are members of the general assembly, members of the *directivas*, delegates of the Word (religious leaders), and extenders of warm hospitality. They have procured the release of three out of four recruits forcibly removed from the community by the army.

Most important, in their weekly meeting they are envisioning a society without armies, one where violence is not an everyday event, where all segments of society are part of a negotiated settlement, where money can be spent on

LAURA JACKSON: *Ciudad Segundo Montes.*

education and health care, where young men can be social-
ized to love rather than to kill and die. They are discussing
the cultural and personal needs for family planning and
celebrating the fact that their men no longer grieve over the
birth of daughters. The results of their discussions are
published in a regular newsletter and disseminated as an
open invitation to transformational thinking.

In many ways life triumphs over death in Segundo Montes. They truly are, as posters in the communities and in San
Salvador proclaim, "the hope that is growing in the east."

B.M.

JOHN GRANT: *Corn and coffins, San Salvador, El Salvador.*

Chapter 6

"THESE ARE SURELY NOT ISOLATED INCIDENTS"

PERSECUTION OF THE VILLAGERS AND THEIR SUPPORTERS

There are many success stories connected with the repatriation movement. There are also tragedies. For after all that these refugees suffered in the original campaigns that drove them out of their homelands, after all that they endured in exile, after all of the efforts they put forth to obtain the permission and the means to return to their homelands—there are still incidents in which they are being persecuted by the army and harassed by the Salvadoran government. At times, their villages are invaded by army personnel without warning. There are reports of women being raped and of religious leaders, teachers, health care workers, and *directiva* members being subject to arrest, interrogation, and torture for up to 72 hours, without a single charge being levied. Food supplies are often intercepted on roads leading into the villages . Villagers going out for food may be subject to detention and interrogation.

Why is this so? While it is true that the Salvadoran government grudgingly gave the refugees from Honduras permission to return to their villages, the *army* never sanctioned repatriation. They claim that the presence of *campesinos* in areas that were formerly free fire zones impedes their pursuit and attempted eradication of the FMLN. In addition, one might well argue that the army *and* the government of El Salvador are threatened by the organization, hopefulness, and assertiveness of poor people whom they have traditionally sought to intimidate and control.

This chapter includes a first-person account of an international arrested and held by the Treasury Police as he was leaving the repopulated villages to return to San Salvador. His treatment was better than that received by most Salvadorans under arrest, but it far exceeded the "crime" of an overextended visa.

Copapayo, El Salvador, December 1987

"THE RELIGIOUS. . . HAVE BEEN GETTING THREATS. . . THESE ARE SURELY NOT ISOLATED INCIDENTS"

People from the Ministry of the Interior (Salvadoran government) paid a visit, to bring "gifts" of macaroni and clothing. The community said they would accept them, only without strings attached. They also went around and talked with people, asking many questions. Not all the people knew they were coming, so they wound up giving some information which could be very dangerous—like names of leaders of the community.

Already one leader in Santa Marta has been captured and beaten. He spent time in the hospital in San Salvador. This is what happens to the leaders in communities like these. Sometimes they have been killed. We pray that it will not happen here.

We've heard other reports, especially from Arcatao, in Chalatenango. There a professor was killed about a month ago, and the religious who have been working in the area (also in San Jose las Flores) have been getting threats, threats on their lives by the military. I know the priest who works there. He's a wonderful man, very dedicated to serving the poor and risking his life to be present there when he's been told to leave several times.

Most recently, a woman was raped by several Salvadoran soldiers in Arcatao. An attempted capture took place at Guarjila, in the same area. Since internationals were there, the capture was aborted. These are surely not isolated incidents. Every day these types of things are happening in different places—not to mention in the city.

M.G.

RENATO CARMADA: *The military makes a routine visit to a repatriated village.*

"THE GOVERNMENT IS WAGING PSYCHOLOGICAL WAR TO DISLODGE US"

Alejandro is joined by Felix in telling about the impact of government repression: On January 17th two helicopter gunships shot up 19 houses (we see the bullet holes in the roof), and on March 15th another aerial strafing damaged nine houses. People have been crippled by mines planted in cornfields; we see two one-legged men. One mine killed a child. Another child was killed by a grenade. These were no accidents but proof that "the government is waging psychological war to dislodge us. But no matter what, we will remain firm here."

What does the village want? Cristiani's victory will not lead to peace; he has already threatened to bomb the repopulated zones. "As a village board, we ask international solidarity and that the US not renew military aid. We have had enough of war to slaughter peasants, workers, and students."

A.D.

"THEY BEGAN TO REBUILD... AFTER FIVE DAYS THE ARMY CAME"

The people of Teocinte said that at first they were glad to be in their country, but, once here, many difficulties followed. The place had been desolate and totally destroyed—mined. They began to rebuild, but after five days the army came. From September to December they searched each house (some seven times), asking each household why they came from Mesa Grande, why they didn't go where the government wanted them to go. Two people narrowly missed being struck by bombs in September. Villagers report:

The army claimed that the medicines in our clinics were not for us but for the guerrillas (our clinic in fact had more meds than the army clinics). They attempted to take the meds from us, but the women of the town surrounded the clinic and would not let the soldiers leave with the medicines.

In February the Atlacatl Battalion came and occupied the town for a week. They left the buildings open that were housing the horses, and we lost one mule. The planes were strafing outside the community. We had been working on our installation of water pipes for three months when the army came, and we had to decide whether to continue or not with

RENATO CARMADA: *Here village children observe Salvadoran soldiers working on their guns. A North American visitor notes: "When the military came to [a repopulated town], only months after settlement, they offered them arms for civil patrol. The community clearly decided in a town meeting: No, if we have arms, someone will attack us. If they attack us, then we will have to attack back. No, we will not have arms." M.C.S.*

them here. We decided we could not stop working every time the army came and continued in secret to carry the 50-pound pipes up the mountain and down the other side to get the water into town. We now have showers and drinking water in several spigots. Since May the troops have come by often but haven't done any searches.

There have been seven captures. Last December a man bringing powdered milk from the Archdiocese was captured by the Fourth Brigade and tortured, then taken to the National Guard in San Salvador. The Church and others intervened, and he was released after 72 hours. (If someone sees you being captured and you confess to no crimes, the army is legally required to bring you before a judge after 72 hours. If you are found to be clean, you are released.) In February six people were captured because they were coming into the repopulated villages with two food trucks. Five were detained for 72 hours. Carmen was sent to the National Guard where she was verbally abused and beaten so badly she vomited blood. She was pressured to confess that she was getting orientation from the FMLN. Due to paid ads in the paper, the National Guard became afraid she was well known and might die on their hands, thus causing a problem for them. So they sent her to a private clinic.

G.W.

San Salvador, El Salvador, November 1989

"A MAN DRESSED IN CIVILIAN CLOTHING WITH A BLACK CLOTH HOOD OVER HIS FACE WAITED FOR ME"

Tim Lohrentz was picked up by the Salvadoran army on November 2nd as he left the repopulated area, after "accompanying" the fourth repatriation from Mesa Grande. His account picks up after he was transferred to the Treasury Police. [Ed.]

The guard led me to a cell. It was dark. Maybe five feet by eight. There was a black foam mattress on the floor and a toilet. A three-by-eight-inch slot was the only opening in the cell door. He placed metal handcuffs around my wrists, then left.

Five minutes later he returned, threw some clothes on the floor, and took off my handcuffs. He told me to change my clothes. I did, putting on the camouflage shorts and a green t-shirt. He came back and bound up all of my clothes, including my boots, and took them away. When he came back, he put the handcuffs back on me, but this time in back. Then he placed a blindfold over my eyes. I could see a little light below me but that was all. I felt very vulnerable.

The jailer muttered at me, asking what church I belonged

to. *"Evangélica,"* I replied. I knew enough not to say Mennonite. "If you are evangelical, where are your tracts?" (I was not in El Salvador to convert anybody, although he would have been a good first case.) Then in his darkest voice he said, "You thought you could sneak through behind the other three. (*Three other members of the international delegation accompanying the fourth repatriation had been arrested the day before.* [Ed.]) You should have known you would be caught. Why were you accompanying the guerrillas?"

"We were accompanying refugees."

"Vamos a matarles." ("We're going to kill them, or you"— it translates both ways.)

As he left, I asked him for water. He ignored me. I was about to faint. I had to drink. The tank of the toilet was open. I ducked my head in and took a big swallow. The water was so refreshing. I was still alive.

Later I was lying on my stomach on the mat. My wrists were hurting badly. *"Parado!"* he shouted. I got up. (*Parado* means standing or stand.) I stood for a moment. I was too weak and had to lie down again. I didn't hear anyone. It must be safe. I almost fell asleep. *"Parado!"* he shouted again. *"Parado!"* I knew he meant business. This time I stayed up. I stood leaning against the wall.

I don't know how much time passed. I thought about my CRIPDES friends who were held and tortured here for over 48 hours in April. I wondered if they were in these cells or some other room. Someone came to the cell. He had a different voice. He led me out. Where were they taking me? "This is it—just don't put me in a room with that jailer," I

thought. He led me down the same hall I had been brought through before. A man told me to sit down and be comfortable.

Four or five men were milling about me. They talked in low voices. I could hear cell doors open and close. Soon they took off the handcuffs and then the blindfold. I almost felt human again. Then I knew that they would do nothing to me. I saw one or two Salvadorans being pushed into cells. Two Treasury policemen took a record of my fingerprints. They did my mug shots. Then, to my dismay, they put the handcuffs back on behind my back as well as the blindfold. They led me to a cell. Out of the corner of the blindfold I could see a Salvadoran being led down the hall. He also had on jail clothes, a blindfold, and handcuffs. He was small, maybe 5'3," and quiet.

After a couple of minutes, they led me back to where I had just been in the hall and took off the blindfold. A man dressed in civilian clothing with a black cloth hood over his face waited for me. He was average height and from the little of his face that I could see, he seemed to have an average complexion for a Salvadoran. He went through the same two forms used previously: the personal data form and the physical features form. He would peer out of his hood to see what type of mouth, nose, eyes, etc. I had and then record it on the form.

"I have already done this," I thought. His only purpose in interrogating me was to intimidate me. So I acted very unintimidated, although he must have been a death squad member.

The last few minutes I was held I heard loud screams and shouts coming from the other cells. I also heard noises that sounded like a fist hitting flesh. One high voice seemed to shout: "Leave me alone!" "Leave me alone!" I wasn't sure if there was one or two people being held. But I am sure that they were being tortured. I didn't want to listen. It was too hard. I could do nothing.

My last "adventure" was entering the US at Houston. The embassy must have called ahead to alert customs because they had the six people returning from our delegation on a list. Four men, three of us just released from the Salvadoran Treasury Police, were interrogated by agents in a closed room for up to ten minutes each. It was more intimidation. The questions they asked implied we had bad motives for visiting El Salvador and that we were not loyal to our country. The US government does not want us visiting El Salvador and the repopulated communities.

T.L.

ROSITA*

by Tim Lohrentz

Rosita,
I found out it was you in the PH [Treasury Police]
I wish to ask your forgiveness
for I left even while you were screaming.
I heard the fists hitting your body,
and your resistance.
Rosita,
because I am white they let me go.
Because I was born in this country "America,"
because some god remains on the side of the rich,
I was released, but you were not.
That man, the one with the black hood,
did he interrogate you too?
Did the evil jailer tell you he would kill you?
Did they give you food or water?
And what about the *capucha*? [the lime hood]
Rosita,
you are now free.
But I am still detained
in the belly of this beast.
Faces become barricades; the stores build walls.
Here the screams are silent
and the resistance even more so.

*A young student failed to come home after the funeral march for the death of ten people killed in the bomb blast at the FENASTRAS office, Thursday, November 2nd. The Treasury Police finally admitted holding her, and on November 6th she was consigned to the women's prison. She was held longer than the 72-hour detention limit, interrogated, beaten, and mistreated. After an investigation, she was released by the judge.

—from CUANES Newsletter

Corral de Piedra (renamed Communidad Ignacio Ellacuria), El Salvador, February 1990

"COME WITH ME—THERE ARE DEAD AND WOUNDED IN CORRAL!"

I awoke on February 11th, as I have so many mornings in the last two months, to the sounds of combat nearby. Shortly thereafter I heard helicopters arriving, and then the A-37 fighter bombers. I kept stepping outside my house to watch—the helicopters circling, strafing, rocketing; the two bombers climbing and diving in huge arcs.

There was a lull in the fighting, and I went back inside to my Sunday morning housecleaning. Within a few minutes I heard a jeep roar up, honking, and then the voice of my friend who has been living in Corral de Piedra since early December: "Come with me—there are dead and wounded in Corral!" I thought for a moment that she meant government soldiers or FMLN combatants.

"Not civilians?" I asked. "Yes, civilians and lots of them," she answered, as I grabbed the emergency equipment I kept in my house. I called to one of the health promoters who lived nearby to come with me. As we raced back in the jeep we passed another car, driven by another volunteer church worker in the area, carrying four of the most severely wounded to the local hospital in Chalatenango.

We arrived in Corral de Piedra to a scene of anguish and confusion: friends and family standing, staring, sobbing. The wounded had been carried to some nearby shacks. While the health promoters and other volunteers from the community helped the wounded into the jeep and the Guarjila cooperative's truck, which had arrived to assist us, I went to look at the house the rocket had hit, and the dead within it. The two vehicles then proceeded toward the hospital. We stopped briefly in Guarjila so that I could get my identification papers. To my amazement and utter horror, as I walked back toward the jeep, a C-47 (a huge, lumbering plane) flew over. It began to strafe while still over Guarjila and continued its firing as it flew toward Corral de Piedra, even as we continued with our evacuation of the wounded.

At the hospital, I tried to make sure that everyone was appropriately treated and also to gather the names and ages of the wounded and of those who had died. Two women and a 13-year-old boy were quickly transferred to the public hospital in San Salvador. One man, two women, and four children were admitted to the hospital in Chalatenango. Five children were treated and released. One child, a four year old, needed to be transferred to the children's hospital in San Salvador and there was no ambulance to transport him. So I took him in the jeep, his IV bottle hanging from the jeep's roll bar. We took with us as well a beautiful four-month-old baby who had been released after her head wounds were sutured. Although her wounds were superficial, she seemed lethargic, and there was no one at hand to care for her. It was her father and two-year-old sister, along with three other children, who had died a few hours before, and her mother was one of the wounded in the ambulance en route to San Salvador.

—A Religious Worker

JOHN GRANT

PART IV

ACCOMPANIMENT

JOHN GRANT: *An international visitor meets with a Co-madre taking refuge in the National Cathedral after being beaten and tear-gassed at a demonstration.*

Chapter 7

"I WILL COME AND GO WITH YOU"
STORIES OF INTERNATIONALS

There are many "places" we can be. We can be in our homes, trying to create little islands of sanity and hope in an insane and despairing world. We can be in our churches, trying to make the important and difficult connection between a God of justice and a world of injustice. We can be in City Hall, working for better local conditions for the poor, the alien, the homeless. We can be in Washington, pressuring for a humane foreign policy, and protesting when inhumane foreign policies are enacted—as they usually are.

There is another "place" we can be. It is alongside the victims—not trying to strategize on their behalf, or propose our solutions for their problems, or otherwise give them the benefit of our "wisdom"—but simply being there in acts of physical solidarity that are essentially the bones and sinew of spiritual solidarity. We can do this in our neighborhoods, our churches, our towns, our nation's capital.

We can also do it in El Salvador.

From the Salvadorans themselves has come a plea that we "accompany" them on their return to the homelands from which they have been ruthlessly and murderously evicted by US-backed troops. The returnees are not so much trying to make a political or social or economic statement as they are trying to make a human statement. It goes: These are our lands, our homes, our farms, our villages. We are entitled to dwell in them. We intend to do so.

Of course, in a complex (and fallen) world, a human statement is also a political, social, and economic statement. It is also a theological statement, since it is dealing with the ultimate issues of life and death. And the plea that accompanies the statement—go with us on this journey—is a theological plea, whether couched in theological language or not.

—from "A Theological Reflection on Accompaniment"
by Robert McAfee Brown

PETER ROBERTSON: *An international with a survivor of the Sumpul River massacre.*

San Salvador, El Salvador, November 1989

"THE THING IS NOT TO LET YOUR FEAR DO YOUR THINKING BUT TO THINK OVER YOUR FEAR"

The North American delegation that arrived in early November right after the fourth return, intending to visit the repopulated communities, had a great deal of trouble obtaining a safe conduct pass to go into the conflicted area. [Ed.]

We had several choices: to return to the High Command of the army and try again for a safe conduct pass on Monday; to go without the permit and thereby risk arrest and detention; to stay in San Salvador and meet with more representatives of the community groups; or to make it politically costly for the military High Command to have denied our safe conduct pass.

Some of our reactions were fear of the unknown, and fear of being separated. But Roberto, our guide, told us, "Don't let fear stop you. You *will* be fearful; the thing is not to let your fear do your thinking but to think over your fear."

He visited the CRIPDES office and returned with new information: European delegations don't even bother asking for permission. We decided to leave at 2:00 a.m. from some place more obscure than our hotel. In case of a roadblock, we would return via the Chalatenango Convent. All agreed to go.

We checked out of the hotel at 2:00 a.m. and walked down the street to a restaurant to meet our van for the ride to Guarjila. The driver and his friends drove through San Salvador down dark, back streets to avoid detention, and then turned into the main highway to the Colima Bridge. We were stopped once and asked to turn off our lights. It was a moment when most of us felt we would not make it, but we did. We arrived at Guarjila at about 5:00 a.m. A woman passerby took us up to the community kitchen and lodge. Some took naps as we waited for the sun to rise and breakfast to be prepared. Although we were not expected, we were warmly welcomed.

S.E.S.

Mesa Grande, Honduras, August 1988

"I WILL COME AND GO WITH YOU"

The bus ride from the camp to the border on the second return was a time for building relationships. I shared a seat with two little girls and a tiny boy, who were three of the six children that belonged to Luis and Maura.

Although there existed a language barrier, we communicated in other ways. I showed them a picture of my family to let them know that I had children of my own. A granola bar went a long way in making friends. An offer of a sweet corn cake in return indicated that I was getting through. What had begun as expressions of anxiety and tension at sharing a seat with the large North American man soon settled into a relaxed sharing of pleasant looks, an occasional touch of the arm, or a mutual exclamation at seeing something beautiful. We were becoming friends at an important moment in their lives, and I'm sure they knew that I had come to help. What was true for me was equally true for the others in our delegation. It was a significant part of the process to become human as well as a symbol.

(*This delegation, like all of them, encountered considerable resistance from the Salvadoran government.* [Ed.]) Who were we? Priests, nuns, social workers, a Baptist and an Episcopal minister, a Jewish Rabbi. Several of us didn't even speak Spanish. It was not we as people who were a threat, but rather our support of the refugees and the support we represented in the United States. We were breaking through the cracking facade of democracy in El Salvador, and the very fact that the government would go to great lengths to denounce our presence and our purpose verifies that fact.

In returning to our bases at home, we carry an obligation to tell the story of a truly profound experience. An experience of love and bravery and courage. An experience which has touched all of us to the core.

In observing this modern Exodus, we have seen in a

RENATO CARMADA: *A North American walks with a large caravan of refugees back to El Salvador from Honduras. Another visitor commented: "I felt very much like I was part of a historical process and played a significant, constructive role in a rare experience, so intense and concentrated." E.K.*

dramatic way the hand of God as it has touched the lives of the people of Mesa Grande and as it has touched each one of us as well.

Carlos, a boy of about 14 years who came to mean a great deal to all of us in the delegation, is one of the 5,000 people who will remain in Mesa Grande. He recognized Mary Jane as among those who had been at the first repatriation.

On the morning we were leaving Mesa Grande, Juan Carlos slipped his small hand into Mary Kay's and looked squarely into her kind and gentle face and said, "María, when will you return?"

And she, speaking for all of us in one way or another, smiled at him as only she can smile and said, "When you go home, Carlos. When you do go home, I will come and go with you!"

M.L.M.

HARVEY FINKLE: *A US visitor assists in the dismantling of a camp building.*

Mesa Grande, Honduras/Teocinte,
El Salvador, October 1989

"PHYSICALLY THIS WAS A HARD JOURNEY FOR AN OLD LADY, BUT IT WAS A PRICELESS ONE"

I had come to Mesa Grande on a delegation in August 1989, which helped with the repatriation of the fourth return. I came back in October to take part in the accompaniment. We marched out of the camp on October 17th and arrived in San Marcos that evening. I was one of the fortunate ones who was able to remain with the returnees in the pavilion through the hunger strike and the encounters with the soldiers.

Physically this was a hard journey for an old lady, but it was a priceless one. I will never forget those people. It was like taking part in the Exodus 3,000 years ago. The Lord is still leading his people. The Church is alive and well in El Salvador, and it is living the life Christ asked us to live. Now each time I say the Lord's Prayer, it has a deeper meaning.

J.F.R.

Corral de Piedra (renamed Communidad Ignacio
Ellacuria), El Salvador, February 1990

"THE WOMEN AND CHILDREN... LITERALLY TOOK US BY THE HAND"

I was part of a religious delegation sent to interview survivors of the air force attack on February 11th and to celebrate a memorial mass for the dead. Yet when I stood surrounded by 100 or so of the women and children of the village, who had come to the army checkpoint where we had been denied passage, two United States military advisors stood with members of the Salvadoran army, blocking our way, and told me that I was an "ugly American" who should go home and stop making trouble. They said that they had been working with the Salvadoran army since 1984, and were sure that they could be trusted. This is the same army who had ordered the two-hour helicopter rocket and machine gun strafing attack against this refugee village, only recently resettled by the United Nations from refugee camps in Honduras.

Surrounded by the women and children of the community who had come to escort us, nine of us were able to slip through the military cordon. Three hours later, the commanding colonel agreed to permit the rest of the delegation to join us in Corral de Piedra (and by his action excuse the

BOB PERILLO: *International visitors negotiate with Salvadoran military and US advisors at a checkpoint.*

earlier group's unauthorized crossing of the checkpoint.) At the place where the attack occurred, we interviewed the survivors and celebrated a commemorative mass with them.

The day after that mass in Corral de Piedra, we celebrated another at the Jesuit University in San Salvador. Afterwards, a surviving Jesuit took us to the place where his friends had died, and I witnessed the all too familiar sight of human blood and tissue splattered on a wall by a military out of control.

We returned from El Salvador encouraged by the massive response of people in the United States, whose telephone pressure on US and Salvadoran officials made it possible for us to go where they clearly did not want us to go. In addition, we were deeply moved by the determination of the women and children of the repopulated communities, who literally took us by the hand when we could not find a way to cross the last checkpoint, announcing for the army and the US military advisors and the whole world to hear: "Thank you for your solidarity. Come on. Let's go. All the people of Corral de Piedra are waiting for you." None of us will ever forget that touch—or that walk.

R.M.

San Salvador, El Salvador, March 1990

"THEY HAVE INDEED CHOSEN LIFE"

On March 27th I returned from a pilgrimage to El Salvador with a Catholic delegation from Philadelphia. I have not yet had time to unpack and sort out the images and emotions that flood my mind and heart, so what I briefly share are unprocessed reflections.

El Salvador—a country of contradictions. As in Macbeth's Scotland, "Nothing is but what is not." The serene, flower-scented chapel where rifle fire tore open the heart of an archbishop already called "Saint Romero" by the Christian communities. The peace of the garden where one wall still bears the stains of Jesuit blood and brains. The orderliness and courtesy of the Office of the High Command where we waited a full day to obtain passes to visit repatriated communities in the countryside and where decisions are made to bomb those same communities. San Salvador, the crowded capital, which, aside from omnipresent soldiers with rifles, appears fairly normal by day but which at dusk grows eerily empty and silent. And the beautiful lake country where resettled communities struggle to rebuild their lives under the menacing hum of military helicopters.

In this country of beauty and violence, evil and holiness, fear and hope, where does one find truth? In the faith of

JOHN GRANT: *Visitors to San Jose las Flores.*

Christian-base communities. In the eyes of children who have known more pain and loss in a few years than I have known in a lifetime. In the strength of women who have lost husbands, fathers, children, yet continue to nourish life and hope. In the men who labor with oxen and plow because the military will not permit the transport of the tractor they have purchased. In the ability of a community to pray and sing and dance with us because they have indeed chosen life "that they and their descendants might live."

M.L.

RENATO CARMADA: *A bienvenido (welcoming service) for international visitors.*

EPILOGUE: HARBINGER OF A NEW EL SALVADOR

For the large communities of former Salvadoran refugees who have returned from Honduras to their homeland, a new era has begun—the era of staying home in dignity and peace. No longer "refugees," soon they also will no longer be called the *"repobladores."* Their new, well-organized communities have welcomed many internally displaced persons. As these people continue to join together, the number of repopulated towns and communities grows. Furthermore, through their example of highly motivated community development and grassroots leadership, these towns are modeling a new El Salvador for many traditional provinces.

In deciding to repatriate and rebuild their destroyed villages, the people of Mesa Grande, Colomoncagua, and San Antonio camps knew full well that repression continued to prevail in their native country. Indeed they were quite aware that not only had the unjust economic structures of their society remained unchanged, but that a more distinctly right-wing regime had come to power.

However, unlike before, they could now face their adversaries as empowered, closely knit communities with advanced negotiation and survival skills—skills which they had cultivated through the hardships and challenges of the camps. Their cooperative values, acquired production skills, and peaceful political objectives are finding creative new forms of expression within the repopulated towns.

For instance, although it is not unusual for rebuilt towns to be offered arms by the military for the alleged purpose of forming civil patrols, the *directivas*, following the expressed will of the people, consistently decline. They explain that they do not want to be forced into combat under any circumstances. Moreover, they remain consciously committed to developing "zones of peace." Their strategy in this regard is to draw international attention to any serious violation of their human rights through their connections with churches and other humanitarian organizations. They wish to obtain wide support for their peaceful, nonviolent lifestyle, and thereby "to create spaces in which to develop."

When necessary and possible, the towns use such means

as public demonstrations, symbolic masses, newspaper ads, and invitations to international observers to undergird their demands for justice. Their faith, deeply rooted in liberation theology and the example of thousands of martyrs in their country, inspires many of them to be willing to suffer or even to die to gain legal rights for their communities. Since the returns, there have been a number of instances in which crops have been destroyed and fields mined by the military; individual leaders have been tortured, and there have been "disappearances" and deaths as well. Sadly, there have also been direct attacks on groups of citizens, although not on the broad scale of the early 1980s.

The worst of these assaults occurred on February 11, 1990, when the military bombarded Corral de Piedra, a small town of five or six hundred persons, who had arrived only three and a half months earlier from Mesa Grande with the fourth return. As a result of direct rocket fire from several US-made helicopters, four children and the father of one of the children were killed. At least 15 other persons in the same building with those who died were seriously wounded.

While the military tried at first to blame the FMLN, government troops the following day offered the people reparations if they would not give witness to the attack. The people refused and began official court proceedings, demanding that the troops which had perpetrated this massacre be identified and brought to trial. In order to be able to present the necessary physical evidence, they obtained a judicial order permitting them to exhume the remains of some of the deceased. In addition, they collected shrapnel and rocket shells and talked openly with human rights organizations and the press about this atrocity.

Rather than withdrawing in fear from this tragic situation, hundreds of people from neighboring towns rushed to Corral de Piedra to provide support and comfort. The communities then published a large ad in the newspaper of San Salvador inviting all of the people of the region to attend a mass in honor of the deceased and wounded.

At the same time, an invitation to the mass was extended to people from Salvadoran and North American churches and humanitarian groups. Within a few days of the attack, a large international delegation set out for this remote town and, as one might suspect, encountered a series of military roadblocks and other bureaucratic obstacles. But taking their cue from the courage of the villagers they were going to visit, they persevered, and finally were able to celebrate mass in Corral de Piedra. The internationals were deeply impressed both with the progress the people had made in rebuilding their town since their repatriation in November and with their continued determination to succeed—despite the recent brutal attack. The town later in the year changed its name to Communidad Ignacio Ellacuria in honor of the martyred Jesuit.

As illustrated by their organizing prowess in the camps, their successful caravans home, and their well-orchestrated responses to periodic incidences of repression, as described above, the Salvadorans who have returned home from Honduras are clearly writing a new chapter in the history of nonviolent struggle. Yet their actions grow out of a rich heritage of nonviolent action in El Salvador and throughout Central America.* Their victories exemplify the power which seemingly powerless people all over the world have found in overcoming fear, organizing themselves nonviolently, and taking charge of their own lives.

What made it possible for them to do what they did? First and foremost, they have nurtured and strengthened each other as communities in solidarity. Second, they have sought allies, whose interposition has raised the visibility of their situation and the price of action against them. Repeatedly they have invited people of conscience both in El Salvador and in the international community to accompany them and to stand with them peacefully through whatever risks they have needed to take to assert their rights.

Third, while maintaining a respectful negotiating posture, they have found ways of gaining leverage with their opponents, and on some occasions even created splits among them. A particularly interesting example of that is the refugees of Colomoncagua who successfully coupled their interest in leaving Honduras with the interest of the Honduran government in seeing them leave, much to the chagrin of the Salvadoran government and the UNHCR, who were seeking to delay repatriation. As described in Chapter 4, refugee leaders persuaded the Honduran military to provide transportation for them out of the camp and to the Salvadoran border, thereby breaking the impasse that existed at that time.

Fourth, with the signing of the Esquipulas agreements by the presidents of the Central American countries, refugee leaders in the camps were able to create a strategic double-bind or no-win dilemma for the Salvadoran government. For while the government did not want these people to return to their towns of origin, especially in regions of El Salvador which were outside of their total control, they could not risk further international embarrassment by violating the agreements at a time when they were supposed to be giving the appearance of making progress toward "democracy."

Like the African-Americans of the 1960s who integrated lunch counters in the southern states of the US, the Salvadoran refugees have insisted on being taken seriously and testing their legal rights. Despite great obstacles, they have returned to their homes when they deemed the time to be right and necessary. In addition, within the camps and later within their newly rebuilt towns, they have begun to actualize working communities based on cooperation, self-sufficiency, collective effort, and the sharing of resources.

Although the threat of the government's forces remains quite real, the repatriated citizens strive for as much normalcy and productivity as possible. Many of the towns are now several years old and are quite well established, while others are constructing their first buildings and planting their first crops. As a North American church delegate who visited one of the earliest rebuilt towns remarked later: "I knew suddenly as I stepped into this very attractive and well-organized little town why the military feared these people so much . . . it was the people's tranquility, hopefulness, self-sufficiency, and pride. They could no longer be intimidated or beaten down like oxen, as they had been treated for centuries before."

As the people have rebuilt their towns, they have in good biblical tradition first constructed the houses of the widows, the elderly, and the disabled. Generally they have chosen to cluster their houses, rather than to live scattered in the countryside as before where they could be more readily harassed. This close arrangement also facilitates their more cooperative community style. Despite frequent interruption of their supplies by the military, they have reestablished as many of their workshops as possible. Modestly built schools, day care centers, and a few clinics have also been constructed through contributions from churches and international relief organizations.

As was the practice in the camps, basic goods created in the workshops are distributed equitably by need among the villagers. Any remaining goods are taken into the larger town of the province where they are sold in the markets. Proceeds are then reinvested in the workshops.

Further, some 50 percent of the agricultural lands around the towns are managed cooperatively by the entire community. Remaining plots are divided up among individual families for private management. After direct distribution of produce from cooperative lands, any produce that remains is taken to market and proceeds are reinvested in seeds and other supplies. In this general manner, with some variation from town to town, the communities are experimenting with cooperative structures as well as with the rudiments of private enterprise. Reports indicate that they are gradually integrating themselves into the simple market economy of

their region.

Because the towns are denied economic support from the Salvadoran government (which accuses them of being allied with the FMLN) and because the towns have refused to accept aid from organizations such as US AID (because of the political directives attached), infrastructures for economic development have formed around indigenous churches and relief agencies in coordination with the international community and despite government persecution of local leaders. A primary conduit for such funding is CORDES (Foundation for Repopulated and Displaced Communities of El Salvador), which is one of several popular organizations that coordinate and distribute resources to the repopulated villages from various humanitarian and development agencies. CORDES accepts project proposals from many towns in the northern and eastern provinces, including projects for agricultural production of rice, beans, corn, and vegetables; for artisan production of shoes, furniture, clothing, etc.; and for day care programs, women's workshops, medical clinics, and community stores.

Together with Diaconia—the ecumenical body of Catholic and mainline Protestant churches of El Salvador which communicates with the international religious community and other NGOs—CORDES encourages trade within the region and seeks to counteract the government's frequent attempts to isolate the villages. CORDES also promotes curative and preventive health care as well as education and pastoral care programs. Lastly, it serves as an intermediary for promoting contacts between the indigenous communities and sister cities in other countries.

Over the years CORDES has demonstrated great care in trying to divide its very limited resources as equitably as possible among the many communities who need help and who submit proposals. Once a decision is made to award funds to a project, regional and local community representatives meet to develop a concrete management plan. Money is then distributed in stages for purposes of accounting and to reduce the possibility of the army's confiscation of significant resources, as has been done in the past.

Undoubtedly the role of the international community in providing material aid and ongoing accompaniment will be crucial even after an effective settlement of the civil war occurs. In response to the direct appeals of the former refugees of Mesa Grande, the Going Home Campaign—developed in 1987 as a joint project of the SHARE Foundation (Salvadoran Humanitarian Aid, Research and Education Foundation), the Interfaith Office on Accompaniment, and CRECEN (Central American Refugee Committee)—has done an extraordinary job of communicating the needs of the Salvadorans to others. Through this campaign, literally hundreds of ordinary US citizens and clergy people from Catholic, mainline Protestant, and Jewish congregations have traveled to El Salvador and Honduras to learn for themselves about these communities. In turn, these "delegates" have, within their own churches and communities, formed active local committees which educate many others, including their political representatives, and raise funds for social and economic projects within the repopulated towns. In ad-dition, the SHARE Foundation itself, which was founded in 1981, has raised over two-and-a-half million dollars in humanitarian aid for emergency relief and development projects in displaced and repopulated communities throughout El Salvador. In addition to its humanitarian aid work, the SHARE Foundation also facilitates sister relationships between US faith-based communities and communities in El Salvador.

Voices on the Border, a Washington-based humanitarian agency, has provided highly effective support for the returning Salvadorans, including accompaniment for all 8,400 persons from the Colomoncagua camp, who between November 18, 1989 and March 3, 1990 successfully returned to the province of Morazan where they built a new town named Ciudad Segundo Montes in honor of the recently martyred Jesuit priest. Along with their connections to North American religious and humanitarian groups, Voices on the Border has also forged ties with many groups in Canada, Scandinavia, Germany, Spain, and other parts of Western Europe, who in turn have organized delegations for accompaniment.

As the people of the repopulated towns have experienced increasing success in the establishment of productive and self-sufficient communities (which is their goal), a basic platform of demands—a kind of "Bill of Rights"—has emerged. These rights include: (a) that there be full *access* to the towns, e.g., that tools, seeds, supplies, and all necessary materials be allowed in, and that the residents and anyone else, including international visitors, be allowed to come and go safely without incident; (b) that the military not be allowed to enter and move directly through the towns, in particular that all community spaces be completely demilitarized; (c) that popular groups be allowed to organize and to advocate or lobby without intimidation or reprisal; (d) that formal elections be held in the towns and provinces which allow for a truly democratic, pluralistic process of governance; and (e) that all military aid from the US end.

Clearly these people are asserting that they want a political settlement between the hostile factions of their country, which have been at war for so long. However, they want it to be a just peace and know that it will not simply happen on its own. Rather, they are committed to assisting the peace process through actualizing productive, nonviolent communities that respect everyone's rights. In this sense the people are indeed harbingers of a new El Salvador. No longer content to wait for happiness after death, they are striving with the full moral force of their communities to experience justice, and, as many of them would say, the Kingdom of God on this earth as well.

V.C.

*See:

Parkman, Patricia. *Nonviolent Insurrection in El Salvador: The Fall of Maximiliano Fernandez Martinez.* Tucson: University of Arizona Press, 1988.

Parkman, Patricia. The Tradition of Urban Nonviolent Action in Twentieth-Century Latin America," *Civilian-Based Defense: News and Opinion,* 5 (September/November 1988), 1-4.

Relentless Persistence: Nonviolent Action in Latin America, edited by Philip McManus and Gerald Schlabach. Philadelphia: New Society Publishers, 1990.

JOHN GRANT: Village folksinger and children, Santa Marta, December 1987, three months after repopulation.

JOHN GRANT: *Lutheran Bishop Medardo Gomez speaking at a March 1989 rally, sponsored by the Permanent Committee for a National Debate, San Salvador.*

CLOSING REFLECTIONS:
REPATRIATION—IN SEARCH OF THE PROMISED LAND

Medardo Gomez, Lutheran Bishop of El Salvador for the past three years, took up the prophetic voices silenced with the murder of Oscar Romero ten years ago. He has paid dearly, as have many Christians in El Salvador who have spoken out against injustice. There are only 6,000 Lutherans in the predominately Catholic country, but Gomez is an ecumenical spokesperson in his criticism of El Salvador's government and in his defense of war victims from all sides of the political spectrum.

In El Salvador such sympathies are the kiss of death. Death came stalking Medardo Gomez on November 16, 1989, now known as Bloody Thursday. It was the day a domestic worker, her daughter, and six Jesuit priests were murdered.

Medardo Gomez was out that day, but 14 of his staff members were arrested. He reports:

"After Bloody Thursday, I visited the refugee camps of Mesa Grande, Honduras. There the refugees told me, 'Bishop Gomez, we want peace.' I asked them why they asked me for peace: 'I cannot bring you peace.' But they responded, 'No, you can bring us peace, Bishop Gomez. You can travel to the United States. Tell our Christian brothers and sisters there that we want peace."

D.R.

The Exodus is the story of how a people searches for better living conditions, for what in the Bible is called the "Promised Land," the land flowing with milk and honey.

Such a search is only accomplished by taking the arduous way. Indeed, it can only be understood by those who join in the search. Christian people, under the inspiration of the Word of God, have always wanted to transform their lands, blessed by God with their children, into the promised land flowing with milk and honey.

On the road of Exodus, one realizes the story of salvation: God with us. The people, accompanied by God, have

SCOTT WRIGHT: *Arcatao, August 1989.*

achieved tremendous conquests and have defeated their pursuers. The sea has opened before the passage of the people, those who are looking for their liberation, leaving behind those enemies who have oppressed and enslaved the poor.

The journey of the exodus in Central America, especially in El Salvador, includes several stages. First of all, the people have united and organized themselves to find solutions to their problems in their own communities; and they continue to unite and organize in a search for life—indeed, a life of dignity.

The people unite and organize because they have been persecuted, beaten, tortured, and forced into exile. The people unite and organize also in order to recover more effectively their rights.

The repatriation of the return of the refugees is another stage of the exodus of the people of God.

By returning to their beloved fatherland, especially under unsafe conditions, they are transforming this event into a pilgrimage of the children of God. Their returning in the form of a march becomes a demonstration of faith. Their people return with high morale, hoping that everything is going to be better. They intend to reconstruct their lives with love and faith. They have learned how to live together, to cry together, and to laugh together.

The representatives of the Churches symbolize God's presence, by giving courage to the people. At the same time, the presence of the Church leaders imparts to the people a spirit of strength and pastoral comfort.

During the trip, which includes the years spent in the refugee camps, they left behind many weaknesses. They have freed themselves from dissentions; in fact, they have so learned how to live together and to trust in each other, that they have accomplished great victories together.

For the refugees, the inward journey has transcended the actual physical return to their beloved fatherland. In their native land they will continue their pilgrimage, until they will arrive one day definitively—in the promised land, the land flowing with milk and honey.

—Bishop Medardo Gomez
translated by Enrique Fernandez

JOHN GRANT: *Man with bucket, Santa Marta, December 1987.*

GLOSSARY OF SPANISH TERMS AND ACRONYMS

ACNUR — the Spanish acronym for the United Nations High Commission on Refugees

ARENA — Nationalist Republican Alliance, the political party presently in power in El Salvador and historically responsible for the formation of death squads

atole — a traditional drink made of corn

bienvenido — welcoming

barrios — neighborhoods

bastante — enough

bodega — warehouse

CARITAS — a Catholic relief agency (in Latin the word means love)

campesino — a peasant farmer

capucha — the lime hood, an instrument of torture; a canvas bag filled with lime or cement that is placed over the head of the victim while he/she is being beaten

CCR — Chalatenango Committee for Repopulation

CEDEN — a coalition of evangelical groups in Honduras

cedula — government-issue identification papers, required at all times for all Salvadoran citizens but often denied to refugees

chapulin — tractor

CNR — National Committee for Repopulation

Co-madres — an organization made up of mothers of the "disappeared"

comandantes — military leaders

compadres — comrades

compañeros — companions

conscientización — the process by which social consciousness is engendered

CORDES — Foundation for Repopulated and Displaced Communities of El Salvador

CRECEN — Central American Refugee Committee

CRIPDES — Christian Committee for the Displaced of El

Salvador

CUANES — Christian Urgent Alert Network of El Salvador

despedida — a farewell

Diaconia — ecumenical body of Catholic and mainline Protestant churches in El Salvador

directiva — an elected town council

FDR — Democratic Revolutionary Front, the political ally of the guerrilla army (FMLN)

FECCAS — Christian Federation of Salvadoran Peasants

FENASTRAS — National Trade Union Federation of Salvadoran Workers

FPL — Popular Liberation Forces

FMLN — Farabundo Marti National Liberation Front

guerrillas — members of an armed opposition

internacionalistas — internationals, the term used by Salvadorans for North Americans who are recognized to be independent of US foreign policy objectives

lamina — galvanized metal roofing

machismo — assumed male superiority

manzana — somewhat more than an acre of land

mesa — plateau

NGOs — non-governmental organizations

PADECOMSM — Community Development Council of Morazan

parado — standing/stand up

pilas — concrete basins

Policia Hacienda — Treasury Police

repobladores — repopulated persons

retorno — a return

saludo — greeting

SHARE — Salvadoran Humanitarian Aid, Research and Education Foundation

tabla — board

Tripartita — a commission of the Honduran and Salvadoran governments and the UNHCR

Tutela Legal — the human rights organization of the Catholic archdiocese of San Salvador

US AID — United States Agency for International Development

UTC — Union of Rural Workers

IDENTIFICATION OF CONTRIBUTORS

The idea for this book was conceived in the fall of 1989, as a project of the Oscar Romero Interfaith Center in Philadelphia in association with Interfaith Office on Accompaniment and the SHARE Foundation.

The **working committee** consisted of:

VIC COMPHER (V.C.)—an author in the area of family-based social services, and a social work supervisor with a public agency in Philadelphia.

BETSY MORGAN (B.M.)—an author in the area of Third World poverty and social responsibility, and a professor of writing and literature at Eastern College in St. Davids, Pennsylvania.

(Vic and Betsy served as project-coordinators and co-editors of the book.)

LAURA JACKSON (L.J.)—a radio producer with National Public Radio in Philadelphia, and a freelance producer of documentary films. She functioned as contributing photographer and as photography editor of the book, and is currently working on a film with Betsy Morgan about repatriation.

JOHN GRANT—a professional photographer (on staff at Widener University in Chester, Pennsylvania) and a writer of fiction. He functioned as contributing photographer and photography consultant for the project.

PATRICIA PARKMAN—an author and historian who has published in the area of nonviolent activism in Latin America, and a staff worker for Peace Brigades International. She served as consultant on historical and political issues.

Other persons who consulted with the editors on matters of historical and political accuracy were: PHILLIP BERRYMAN, noted author on Latin American history and liberation theology; JOSÉ ESCOBAR, Executive Director of the Interfaith Office on Accompaniment in San Francisco; and PEDRO MENENDEZ, Philadelphia, Director of the Interfaith Office on Human Rights in El Salvador.

Contributors of Written Materials
(initials included if used in the text)

(V.B.) VIRGINIA BEAHAN—an artist/photographer living in Newtown, Pennsylvania.

ROBERT McAFEE BROWN—a theologian and author who serves on the faculty of the Graduate Theological Center in Berkeley, California.

(R.C.) RENATO CARMADA—a freelance journalist who has written extensively on Salvadoran refugees and currently lives in West Germany.

(P.C.) PACO CASCON—the coordinator for Peace Brigades International in Barcelona, Spain, developing materials and training workers in the areas of nonviolence, human rights, and ecology.

(A.D.) ALAN DAWLEY—a historian of social movements in the United States living in Langhorne, Pennsylvania.

(E.F.) ELIZABETH FRIEDMAN—a graduate student in history at Stanford Univerity in Palo Alto, California.

(S.G.) SANTO GAIRO—a social worker involved in problems of homelessness and affordable housing in Newtown, Pennsylvania.

(M.G.) MARY GIRARD—an activist in peace and justice issues in Chicago, Illinois.

MEDARDO GOMEZ—the Lutheran Bishop of El Salvador and a well-known spokesperson for the struggle for peace and justice.

(D.G.) DAVID GRACIE—an Episcopal priest, working as campus minister at Temple University in Philadelphia, Pennsylvania.

(K.H.) KATHLEEN HAYES—the Director of Publications for Evangelicals for Social Action and Just Life in Philadelphia, Pennsylvania.

(E.K.) ED KINANE—a solidarity worker for Central American issues living in Syracuse, New York.

(E.L.) ELIZABETH LAFOREST—a Sister of Mercy and part-time teacher in adult education and English as a second language, active in peace and justice issues in Detroit, Michigan.

(T.L.) TIM LOHRENTZ—a staff member of the Wisconsin Committee on Central America.

(M.L.) MARIE LUCEY—a Sister of St. Francis and worker in justice and peace for her religious congregation in Philadelphia, Pennsylvania.

(M.L.M.) MARTIN L. MASSAGLIA—pastor of the Royersford Baptist Church in Royersford, Pennsylvania.

(R.M.) RON MORGAN—a woodworker and member of the Going Home Steering Committee in Philadelphia, Pennsylvania.

(J.M.) JACK MUNDAY—a lawyer and theologian who practices law and writes in Ocean City, Maryland.

(J.F.R.) JANE FROH RAMSEY—a retired emergency medical technician who lives in Louisville, Kentucky.

(D.R.) DEE DEE RISHER—an editor with *The Other Side* magazine who lives in Philadelphia, Pennsylvania.

(S.E.S.) SUZANNE E. SATTLER—an Immaculate Heart sister, an attorney specializing in health policy and community economic development in Detroit, Michigan, and President of the Board of Interfaith Office on Accompaniment.

(M.C.S.) MARY C. SLICHER—the director of a housing and advocacy organization for homeless children in Baltimore, Maryland.

(N.V.) NORBERTO VALDEZ—an anthropologist at Western Maryland College, with interests in Third World development and liberation movements, residing in Westminster, Maryland.

(P.W.) PATRICIA WATSON—a Quaker educator and peace activist who works with a food cooperative in Arlington, Massachusetts.

(G.W.) GATEWOOD WEST—a social worker in private clinical practice in Lexington, Massachusetts.

(S.W.) SCOTT WRIGHT—a North American religious who has worked for many years in El Salvador with refugees and displaced persons.

Direct interviews with refugees were conducted by LAURA JACKSON, together with translator MARY REISACHER who worked at the La Virtud and Mesa Grande refugee camps in the early 1980s.

Other Written Material Credits

The introduction to Medardo Gomez in "Closing Reflections" was reprinted with permission from *The Other Side*, 300 West Apsley, Philadelphia, PA 19144. "A Baptism of Fire" in Chapter 1, was reprinted with permission from *Sojourners*, Box 29272, Washington, DC 20017. "The Refugees Were Coming and They Had Better Get Ready" in Chapter 3 was reprinted with permission from *Evangelicals for Social Action*, 10 Lancaster Avenue, Philadelphia, PA 19151. *"Que Viva El Secondo Retorno! Que Viva El Pueblo Refugiado!"* in Chapter 3 was reprinted with permission from *The Witness* magazine, November 1988. The introduction to Chapter 7 is reprinted with the permission of Robert McAfee Brown.

Contributing Photographers

STEVE CAGAN—a socially engaged photographer and critic who lives in Cleveland, Ohio, and teaches photography at Rutgers University. In May 1991, Rutgers University Press will be publishing a book by him and his wife Beth about Colomoncagua.

RENATO CARMADA—(see listing for contributors of written materials).

HARVEY FINKLE—a Philadelphia-based photographer who traveled to Honduras for the project in order to record the fourth repatriation.

JOHN GRANT—(see listing for the working committee).

LAURA JACKSON—(see listing for the working committee).

ADAM KUFELD—a California-based photographer with Central American interests.

RON MORGAN—(see listing for contributors of written materials).

BOB PERILLO—a solidarity activist currently residing in Connecticut.

RICK REINHARD—a Washington-based photographer who has contributed work to the Going Home Campaign.

EDWIN REMSBERG—a photographer also contributing work to the Going Home Campaign.

DODY RIGGS—a Massachusetts-based documentary photographer/writer specializing in projects which focus on economically undeveloped, disadvantaged, and underserviced populations.

PETER ROBERTSON—a photographer living in Austin, Texas, who is involved in the movement for peace with justice and dignity for the people of El Salvador.

PAUL SCIRE—a staff person for the SHARE Foundation for the Going Home Campaign. (The Foundation also contributed other photographs.)

SCOTT WRIGHT—(see listing for contributors of written materials).

All of us—editors, writers, interviewers, photographers, consultants—are honored by and grateful to the many Salvadoran refugees who allowed us to share their stories, and who expressed so eloquently what it means to be human beings living in courageous and compassionate community.

Persons wishing to support the economic development of the repopulated Salvadoran communities may send contributions directly to the following organizations, and may also contact them for more information about accompaniment opportunities:

SHARE Foundation
Box 16, Cardinal Station
Washington, DC 20064
(202/319-5540)

Interfaith Office on Accompaniment
1050 South Vaness Avenue
San Francisco, CA 94110
(415/821-7102)

Voices on the Border
P.O. Box 53081
Temple Heights Station
Washington, DC 20009
(202/332-1421)

NEST Foundation
P.O. Box 411436
San Francisco, CA 94141
(415/864-7755)